Escape from the Central Bank Trap

Escape from the Central Bank Trap

How to Escape From the $20 Trillion Monetary Expansion Unharmed

Daniel Lacalle

BEP BUSINESS EXPERT PRESS

Escape from the Central Bank Trap: How to Escape From the $20 Trillion Monetary Expansion Unharmed

First published in 2017 by
Business Expert Press, LLC
222 East 46th Street, New York, NY 10017
www.businessexpertpress.com

ISBN-13: 978-1-63157-783-3 (paperback)
ISBN-13: 978-1-63157-784-0 (e-book)

Business Expert Press Finance and Financial Management Collection

Collection ISSN: 2331-0049 (print)
Collection ISSN: 2331-0057 (electronic)

Cover and interior design by Exeter Premedia Services Private Ltd., Chennai, India

First edition: 2017

10 9 8 7 6 5 4 3 2 1

Printed in the United States of America.

Dedicated to my love, my wife Patricia and my three children, Jaime, Pablo, and Daniel. You are my life and my inspiration to be better every day. Also to our pet family, Kilda, Blinky, and Ravioli.

Abstract

The financial crisis was much more than the result of an excess of risk. It is essential to understand that the same policies that created each subsequent bust are the same ones that have been implemented in the past years, through Quantitative Easing (QE) to allegedly "solve" this crisis.

In this book, I explain how, through lower interest rates and the artificial creation of money, central banks have created a massive liquidity trap, perpetuating bubbles, incentivizing high debt, and increasing financial risk.

The objective of this book is to present solutions in fiscal and monetary policy that can be implemented today, while at the same time debunking magical solutions offered by some authors, particularly the so-called Modern Monetary Theory. I also explore the impact of monetary expansion on commodities and Emerging Markets, Trump's economic policies, Japan's fight against stagnation, Russia's central bank unique strategy, and the European Union model.

Escape from the Central Bank Trap is about realistic solutions for the threat of zero-interest rates and excessive liquidity. Overcapacity, high debt and perverse incentives to assault taxpayers and consumers are not ingredients of welfare, but of secular stagnation.

The United States needs to take the first step, defending sound money and a balanced budget, recovering the middle-class by focusing on increasing disposable income, and supporting productivity growth. The rest of the OECD will follow. Because supply-side policies work.

Our future does not need to be low growth and high debt. We cannot expect humanity to progress if we enslave future generations with unsustainable debt levels just to perpetuate the imbalances of an inefficient economic model.

Cheap money becomes very expensive in the long run. There is an escape from the Central Bank Trap.

Keywords

Austrian school, debt, economics, financial crisis, inequality, Keynesianism, modern monetary policy, monetary policy, QE, supply side, taxation, Trump, welfare

Contents

Acknowledgment

Thanks to Tressis, Yanire Guillen, and Alvaro Martin, as well as El Español, Hedgeye, CNBC, for the invaluable help in putting together this book and the information therein.

PART I

Creating Money from Nowhere

CHAPTER 1

How Did We Get Here?

"And you may ask yourself—Well … how did I get here?"
(Talking Heads, Once In A Lifetime. Remain In Light)

"Unconventional monetary policy." You might have heard it many times, but it's a misleading term.

What mainstream media and consensus call "unconventional" is and has been the most conventional policy of the past 600 years: to try to solve structural imbalances and macroeconomic problems through inflationary measures; creating money out of thin air.

Printing money, of course, is not exactly what the major central banks have been doing. What they have been doing in the past eight years is more complex. The idea of using the apparently endless balance sheet of a nation's central bank to absorb government bonds and similar instruments to free up banks' capacity and allow them to lend more to Small and Medium Enterprises (SMEs) and families has a logic—but only when it is a temporary measure to provide liquidity, reduce unwarranted risk perception, and return to normal. The idea seemed good at the time. Until the "temporary" and "extraordinary" measures became the norm.

And therein lies the problem. Monetary policy is nothing more than a short-term tool, but it does not solve structural imbalances. At best, as Mr. Mario Draghi, president of the European Central Bank (ECB), reminds every time he speaks, it is a measure that buys time and allows governments and other economic agents to sort out problems, mostly derived from excess debt and poor capital allocation.

But even the most carefully planned program creates significant perverse incentives. The most obvious one is to make the same mistakes repeatedly.

By the end of 2015, more than 25 central banks in the world were following the same path: "Easing," or, lowering interest rates and increasing money supply.

After eight years, more than $24 trillion of fiscal and monetary expansion, and over 650 rate cuts, the balance is certainly disappointing. It was very easy to get in the liquidity trap of endless cheap money, and in this book, we will explore how to escape from it unharmed.

Let us look at the results achieved from years of stimulus and hundreds of rate cuts:

At 3.1 percent, the year 2016 saw the poorest global GDP growth since the crisis.
The U.S. growth is the poorest of any recovery and half of its potential, with labor participation at 1978 levels.[1]
World trade has fallen to 2010 levels.[2]
Global debt has ballooned to an all-time high of $152 trillion, or 225 percent of world GDP.[3]

Rise in government debt as a percentage of GDP from 2007 to 2015:

o United States, from 64 percent in 2007 to 105 percent in 2015
o China, from 35 to 45 percent
o Eurozone, from 65 to 97 percent
o Japan, from 183 to 230 percent[4]

Meanwhile, the largest bubble in bonds ever seen was created, with $11 trillion of negative-yielding bonds issued and high yield at the lowest rate in 30 years.[5]

Yet the media calls this a success.

Are these the results anyone would have expected from a massive monetary stimulus? Clearly not.

---

[1] Labor force participation 62.7% in 2016, growth expectations were halved by the Federal Reserve from January to December 2016.
[2] World Trade Organization (WTO), December 2016.
[3] International Monetary Fund (IMF) Global Outlook.
[4] World Bank, 2015.
[5] Bloomberg, November 2016.

While media and consensus economists were calling for devaluation policies to increase exports, these have stalled;[6] and the boost to global growth ended at the weakest level in decades.

But ... How Did We Get Here?

Through the same measures that we have used to "tackle the crisis."

We got here doing exactly what the media is offering as "the solution"—a massive expansion of credit and money supply. If we ask any economist in the world about the origins of the financial crisis, they will immediately answer pointing out to "excess leverage" and "too much risk" as the causes. However, this is partially true, because those were effects, not causes.

The origin of this crisis,[7] like every other financial crisis in history, was the massive increase in risk generated by manipulating the amount or price of money; in this case, it was lowering interest rates artificially.

Crises are not generated in assets that the public or economic agents perceive as risky, but in those where the consensus is that the risk is very low. In 2008 it was housing; in 2016 it is bonds.

In the origin of all financial crises, we see the stubborn determination of governments and central banks of ignoring economic cycles as if monetary policy will change them—the magical idea that imbalances will be solved by perpetuating and increasing those same imbalances. Excess debt and misallocation of capital are not problems that will be solved by lower interest rates and more liquidity; in fact, those measures simply prolong the same course of action by economic agents.

Low interest rates and high liquidity fuel the fire; they don't extinguish it. At best, the measure should be aimed at helping deleverage and cutting the chain of risk taking while the economy recovers, but that does not happen. The incentive for misallocation of capital is too large.

---

[6] Global exports growth 2010–2016 flat, according to WTO.

[7] Recommended reading: The Origin of Financial Crises: Central Banks, Credit Bubbles, and the Efficient Market Fallacy (October 29, 2008) by George Cooper.

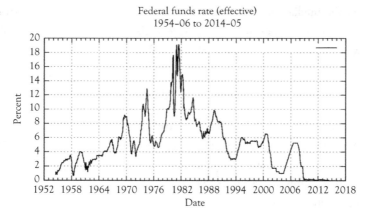

Figure 1.1 Historical chart of the effective Federal Funds Rate. From 2001 to 2006 interest rates were dramatically lowered

Creating money, lowering interest rates, forcing credit growth at any cost, and increasing money supply are the same measures, just with different tools. In the years 2001 to 2008 the excessive risk taking was promoted by central banks and governments' lowering interest rates dramatically;[8] the conduit for debt-fueled growth was the private sector, with the financial system as the facilitator. See Figure 1.1. Money was too cheap to ignore.

After September 11, 2001, the U.S. Federal Reserve began to inflate credit supply to try to prevent an economic crisis. Low interest rates, which reached around 1 percent in 2003, made commercial banks and other financial agents have excess cash to lend even to individuals with poor solvency ratios (what we called "subprime").

The largest originators of these loans were two public-sector entities, Freddie Mac and Fannie Mae. See Figure 1.2. Were the banks reckless and taking unwarranted risk? No. The public and expert opinions were that housing was a safe bet. The safest bet, actually. It was a low-risk and very liquid asset that could be sold at a higher price quickly if the borrower could not meet payments.

---

[8] Since 2008 we have seen more than 650 cuts to interest rates (Alex Dryden at JP Morgan Asset Management).

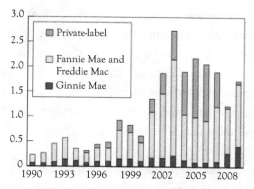

Figure 1.2 Value of mortgage-backed security issuances in $trillions, 1990 to 2009

Source: Securities Industry and Financial Markets Association (SIFMA) statistics.

The process by which this credit was generated violated the traditional principles of bank management. Or did it? Banks invested in long-term assets (mortgages) the funds they received in the form of short-term debt (public deposits), hoping to meet these short-term obligations by repaying in the interbank money markets. The reason to do this was the widespread perception that the asset was liquid and very profitable because the underlying (real estate) demand was virtually inelastic and prices would not drop, and, if they did, it would be by a very small amount.

The result of it was a brutal credit expansion fueled by the relentless message that houses were a secure and ever-rising asset. Like all bubbles, this one lasted longer than any skeptic could have imagined, making even the most doubtful of analysts question their position. Rising demand for credit meant higher housing prices, which in turn led to more risky mortgages and the prospect of higher returns. Liquidity was such that economic and financial agents would absorb any asset, no matter how speculative it was, because the risk seemed inexistent and prices kept rising. It seemed there was never enough supply of home and risky assets.

Household debt went from 100 percent of disposable income to 160 percent, and suitably, house prices doubled.[9]

---

[9] Bank of International Settlements (BIS).

By 2004 many borrowers began to experience difficulties in repaying their loans, but demand remained healthy and house prices were slowing down, but not falling. The bubble was bursting, but the consensus was that it was no real issue. Credit for housing exceeded 20 percent of all outstanding credit. However, by early 2007 reality started to kick in and the chain of nonperforming loans started to explode, as household debt exceeded disposable income by more than 60 percent and thus began a series of massive defaults.

These defaults sank the market value of all the related mortgage loans. Given that banks had to pay for their short-term debts while a substantial part of their income disappeared, a liquidity crisis was generated. As the market value of subprime loans fell further, the liquidity crisis deepened, so much that banks themselves did not want to lend to each other.

The risk of a run on the banks increased, as customers and the general public feared for their deposits.

Central banks decided to come help contain the fire they had created with a massive liquidity injection.

Central banks behaved, again, as the "Pyromaniac Fireman," as I always say.

I remember when Christine Lagarde, then head of the IMF said, "Central banks have been the heroes of this crisis."[10] She completely ignored the role of the same central banks in fueling the housing bubble by slashing interest rates.

The Federal Reserve launched QE1[11] and the mirage of growth and stability through monetary policy emerged. But evidence shows that monetary stimulus simply does not work.

In a report titled "A report card for unconventional monetary policy," Deutsche Bank analyzed in 2016 the impact of "unconventional" monetary policies, quantitative easing (QE), and negative interest rates on the economy.

---

[10] "In many ways, the central banks have been the heroes of the worldwide financial crisis," Lagarde Jackson Hole, Wyoming, 2013.

[11] Quantitative Easing: using the Central Bank balance sheet to purchase government bonds and mortgage-backed securities to free space in banks' balance sheets to improve lending to the real economy.

Studying the impact on manufacturing indexes of these measures from the launch until the end of each unconventional policy, the bank found the following results:

- In eight of the twelve cases analyzed, the impact on the economy was negative.
- In three cases, it was completely neutral.
- The measures only worked in the case of the so-called QE1 in the United States, and fundamentally because the starting base was very low and the United States became a major oil and gas producer.

How do you evaluate if QE and negative interest rates are working? When I discuss this with clients, I sometimes get the response that QE and negative interest rates are working well because the payment systems are running and the financial system still functions. But the issue is not if computers can deal with negative interest rates. The issue is if QE and negative rates have been supporting the economy. The conclusion is that U.S. QE1 had an impact but in all other cases the impact of QE and negative interest rates has been insignificant. And in 8 out of 12 cases, the economic impact has been negative. Once again, there is too big of a burden on monetary policy and it is time for fiscal and structural policy to step up and begin to support GDP growth.[12]

The fact that in eight out of twelve cases the impact was negative speaks for itself.

Would it have been worse if these measures had not been implemented? The debate is open, but I will make my own analysis. Kenneth Rogoff states, "QE was worth taking the added risk entailed by having more short-term debt. But as the recession abates, the calculus of risk and benefit changes."[13]

---

[12] Torsten Slok, Deutsche Bank, "A report card for unconventional monetary policy" November 2016.

[13] Kenneth Rogoff, "Was quantitative easing best way to boost U.S. economy?" March 2015.

My view is somewhat different. I use risk compared to reward and I get to the conclusion that it would not have made much difference compared to a short-term liquidity injection measure targeted exclusively to the banks. The Troubled Asset Relief Program (TARP),[14] which created incentives to restructure banks while at the same time generating profits for the government, would have been more than enough, and the other negatives would have been avoided.

At the end of the day, when we measure the success or failure of a particular policy we must have a clear analysis of the negative and positive effects achieved with it. Assuming that household income and employment would have worsened if such measures had not been implemented is more than questionable. In fact, looking at the examples of both the European Union (EU) and the United States immediately prior to QE and QE1, we can see that the economy had already bottomed out and started to bounce.[15]

Other important factors that help us know if things would have "really" worsened had it not been for monetary stimulus are money velocity, investment (capex or capital expenditure), and debt. While none of them have improved since the implementation of nonconventional measures, we simply cannot assume that they would have deteriorated much more than they have in the past years.

What about inflation? The same. Combating deflation in itself is no evident requirement. But if monetary stimulus of the size and period as the ones implemented does not even do it, the "it would have been worse" argument does not stack up.

Four Trillion for Nothing

"Money for nothing and chicks for free" (Dire Straits, Money For Nothing, Brothers In Arms).

We mentioned before the negatives generated by monetary stimulus. Which negatives?

---

[14] TARP was a program to purchase toxic assets from financial institutions to strengthen the U.S. financial sector. It generated a profit for the government of almost 20 billion US$ from the $426.4 billion invested.

[15] U.S. employment and GDP growth, same with EU.

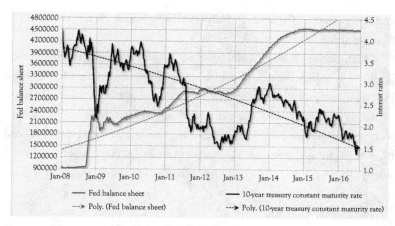

Figure 1.3 Fed Balance Sheet vs. Interest Rates

Source: Realinvestmentadvice, Bloomberg.

Let us remember what was promised to support the massive stimulus plan:

The White House predicted an average growth in the economy of 4 to 4.5 percent, unemployment would drop to 5 percent, and the budget deficit would shrink to a mere 3.5 percent of GDP.

During the Obama administration and the implementation of massive expansionary policies of three QE programs and ultra-low rates (see Figure 1.3), economic growth was a mere average of 1.4 percent. That compares to an average 3.5 percent with Reagan, 3.9 percent with Clinton, and 2.1 percent with Bush Jr.[16]

The recovery growth gap, compared to other recoveries since 1960, has been set at $1.67 trillion. That means the weakest recovery in recent history, as well as an economic growth that has stalled at almost half of the promised growth. The Federal Reserve expected 1.9 percent growth for 2016 going to 2 percent in 2018, the weakest relative to potential and previous recoveries.

All of this is after a massive $4.7 trillion monetary stimulus and $10 trillion in new debt, a fiscal deficit increase of $13 trillion at state, local,

---

[16] Average annual GDP growth.

and federal levels. Public debt ballooned from 48 to 75 percent of GDP. Average annual deficit was 5.2 percent.

Quantitative easing was launched under four premises: provide liquidity to reduce the risk of contagion after the financial crisis; add jobs; inflation; and growth.

Its first objective was clear and worked. Unfortunately, it went from solving a problem of liquidity to creating the largest bubble in financial history: high-yield bonds at the lowest interest rate seen in 30 years, and stocks at all-time highs, exceeding fundamental valuations and real earnings growth.

But job creation was a success. Or was it? Unemployment at 4.6 percent and 9.3 million jobs created. Though good, these employment figures are far from what is expected of the world's leading economy after a $24.7 trillion fiscal and monetary stimulus. Under President Reagan 12.6 million jobs were created; under Clinton, 21 million. Even with massive crisis, Bush Jr. saw 5.7 million jobs created.

On the one hand, more than 11 million people are out of the labor force, leaving the labor participation rate at 1978 levels. Some argue that it is explained by demographics, but that is incorrect. The United States and the United Kingdom have similar demographics; yet the former's labor force participation is almost ten points lower. In addition, labor force participation rate has fallen in almost all segments of age, including the important segment of 25 to 35 years.[17]

A total of 94.6 million working-age Americans are not participating in the system or looking for a job. That shows a labor participation rate of 62.8 percent—not seen since 1978. In addition, the number of U.S. citizens who supplement their income with food stamps has doubled from 20 million to more than 40 million.

Temporary employment stands at 18.2 percent (less than 35 hours per week)—a level that is considered as like recessionary periods. In times of growth, the United States has always had a 16.6 percent lower temporary rate. In the recession of 2001 it was 17 percent and in 2008 the maximum was 20 percent. With the biggest stimulus in history, it has

---

[17] Labor Statistics, November 2016.

only reduced slightly to 18.2 percent, even with the aforementioned poor labor participation.

Since 2009, while national debt has doubled, the average household income in the United States has fallen in all segments (the median of $ 55,000 to $ 54,000 and the poorest segment from $13,000 to $12,000) and real wages continue to be at 2008 levels.

To top it all, in the last five years, the United States' annual productivity growth has been 0.6 percent on average, the poorest since 1978.[18]

Inflation expectations have also been consistently revised down throughout the period.

What is more interesting is that QE has been disinflationary as money velocity has collapsed and capacity utilization remains poor, at 75 percent. The massive creation of money has gone to create huge inflation in financial assets and disinflation in the real economy, laying the grounds for one of the most dramatic imbalances seen between asset classes and industry and consumption since the 70s.

The argument against all this is that "it would have been worse" and that the crisis was too big. None of these arguments work, and sound more like excuses, as other presidents lived through deep crises as well.

But those excuses don't stack up against the fact that the United States created more than half of all the money supply in its history in the past eight years and has seen the longest period with ultra-low rates.

In summary, the Federal Reserve's policy has generated results that range from disappointing liquidity to complete failure in terms of jobs, growth, and inflation—but it leaves behind a massive bubble in financial assets that will not be easily sorted.

"You can do anything you want to do, Do what you want" (Phil Lynott)

"Monetary laughing gas." I have been using this term for a number of years because the effect on the real economy, the healing power of monetary policies is simply a placebo effect. It does not solve the problems of the economy, it just sugarcoats it with the elusive "wealth effect."

What is "wealth effect"? Devaluation policies, massive liquidity, and lowered interest rates do not help the real economy directly; anyone

---

[18] All data from 2008 to 2016 from official figures.

thinking otherwise is simply fooling himself. But the expected result is that stocks will rise, bond yields will fall, asset prices—particularly home prices—will rise, and this will make citizens feel richer. The "wealth effect." It would make sense if not for a small problem—it is utter rubbish.

Less than 10 percent of the wealth of U.S. citizens is in stocks and bonds, and most homeowners have large mortgages. In most OECD countries, less than 6 percent of an average family's wealth is in equities and bonds.

Guess where most of the average citizen's wealth is? In cash.[19] This shows why governments find so appealing the temptation of solving imbalances through devaluation, inflation, and demonetization—eliminating cash, as seen in India, Pakistan, and Venezuela. It is exactly the same as slipping the hand into savers' pockets to pay for the government's lunch. Indebted governments benefit from inflation and increasing money in circulation; savers lose purchasing power and their wealth.

Through massive monetary policies, what governments basically do is erode the middle class's wealth by destroying the value and price of money.

By injecting massive amounts of liquidity into the system, central banks effectively transfer wealth from the savers to indebted governments and to the financial system.

However, most consensus economists will tell you that this is essential to fight deflation.

What is deflation, and is it something negative?

Deflation is, in simple terms, the process by which prices fall.

Deflation is a contraction in the supply of circulated money within an economy, and therefore the opposite of inflation. In times of deflation, the purchasing power of currency and wages are higher than they otherwise would have been. This is distinct from but similar to price deflation, which is a general decrease in the price level, though the two terms are often mistaken for each other and used interchangeably.[20]

---

[19] Average of the OECD is 80 percent.

[20] Investopedia.

But deflation is also caused by technology and by improvements in productivity, so there should be at least a different way to measure inflation and deflation as positive or negative.

For example, a moderate level of inflation can be positive if the rise in prices comes from higher wages, better growth, and a healthier improvement in consumption patterns. It comes as a result of tightening supply and better demand and, most importantly, it does not attack purchasing power as wages improve.

However, when inflation comes from the increase in the price of commodities essential for energy supply, such as oil or coal, and the rise in food prices, it does not generate any positive effect. That is why most economists look at core inflation—excluding food and energy—as a more robust means of analyzing inflation. Additionally, even core inflation rises can be negative if—as we have seen almost every time in the past two decades—real wages do not rise and purchasing power is eroded.

Have you ever seen anyone leaving a supermarket shouting, "Damn, prices have fallen again?" Never.

There has never been a single citizen in the world that has complained about lower prices. Yet consensus Keynesian economists will tell you it's the worst thing in the world.

Why?

Inflation is taxation without legislation.[21]

When inflation rises, debts fall. And the most benefitted are the indebted entities that can increase their prices as well with inflation, because of a semimonopolistic nature. That is, government and crony semimonopolistic sectors, those that many countries love to call "strategic sectors."

It is, therefore, logical, that these entities, particularly governments, do all they can to "combat deflation" even if it is—and *it is*—against the savings and deposits of their own citizens.

However, there is a case to be made for moderate deflation, as George Selgin, professor of economics at the University of Georgia,[22] points out:

---

[21] Milton Friedman.
[22] A Case For Moderate Deflation, Cato Policy Report, May 2003.

Deflation. For many people the word evokes images of the Great Depression, when prices fell dramatically in most of the world. The decline in prices was the counterpart of the collapse in sales, widespread bankruptcies, and the armies of unemployed workers. If a little inflation is the only guarantee against another calamity like that of the thirty, then it is certainly a price that should be paid.

The truth, however, is that deflation does not have to be a recipe for depression. On the contrary, a moderate deflation may be good news, as long as it is the correct type of deflation.

Since the disastrous thirties, economists and central bankers seem to have lost sight of the fact that there are two kinds of deflation-one malignant, the other benign. Malignant deflation, of the type that accompanied the Great Depression, is a consequence of the contraction in spending, corporate profits, and wages. In fact, even in this case, it is not deflation itself which is harmful, but its underlying cause, an inadequate stock of money. The hoarding of money, or its current disappearance (the amount of money in the U.S. economy actually contracted 35 percent between 1930 and 1933), causes demand for goods and services to evaporate. In response, firms are forced to reduce production and lay off workers. Prices fall, not because goods and services abound, but because money is scarce.

Benign deflation is something completely different. It is the result of improvements in productivity, that is to say, times when technological or administrative advances allow the obtaining of greater real quantities of final goods and services with the use of a given amount of land, labor, and capital. Since a rise in productivity is the same as a decrease in production costs, a reduction in prices in the final goods and services due to higher productivity does not imply any fall in the profits of producers or the wages of their workers. The lower costs are matched by lower consumer prices, not by lower wages or revenues. Such deflation—originated in productivity—is good news for the average wage earner.

The case for moderate deflation has been instrumental in the recovery of the EU after the 2008 crisis. The reduction in wages and the employment loss after the crisis were mitigated by price stability, and the strengthening of the currency helped families recover their wealth, mostly accumulated in bank deposits, quickly, before 2012. Had the EU decided to resort to the historical measures of massive competitive devaluations, the impact of higher unemployment with rising prices would have impoverished families further. This is not a counterfactual argument—it is the evidence of years of incorrect monetary policies from the part of peripheral European countries.

Between 1980 and 1996, all peripheral European countries used constant devaluations as a form of trying to improve competitiveness and reduce imbalances. However, despite a devaluation of more than 60 percent to the U.S. dollar, Greek fiscal deficits averaged 7.3 percent of annual GDP deficit in the 20 years before entering the EU, and unemployment multiplied by four.[23]

In Spain, the local currency depreciated more than 50 percent against the U.S. dollar in the same period; public spending doubled in real terms; inflation tripled (an average annual Consumer Price Index (CPI) rate of 7.2 percent); and unemployment did not fall from 15 percent—in fact it was above 20 percent for half of the period.[24]

These projects of competitive devaluations did not work even though national and international conditions were propitious, since the world growth was higher and with much less debt than in 2010–2016.

The crisis of 2008 did not come from lack of stimulus, but from the excess of it.

To look back at the same mistakes made in the past as the solution does not work.

Central banks, in the period before and after the crisis, have played the role of the pyromaniac fireman, creating the conditions for the crisis and offering the same tools to solve it.

For an investor, or somebody interested in economics, there are a few lessons to be drawn, particularly in the face of significant changes in the course of policy making:

[23] Michael Mitsopoulos, *Understanding the Crisis in Greece: From Boom to Bust.* 2011. Palgrave Macmillan.
[24] Juan Rallo, *The Failure of Competitive Devaluations.*

- Always look at real changes in the economy relative to the imbalances created.
- Always analyze the improvements or weakening of the economy relative to the amount of debt accumulated and the changes in microeconomic metrics.
- Always analyze consensus estimates with a critical eye. Consensus and major economic bodies have traditionally missed their estimates due to overly optimistic predictions.[25]
- Being overly pessimistic is as dangerous as being excessively optimistic. Cycles happen, and investors must understand these cycles to profit from expansionary periods without taking them for granted.
- Massive debt and large monetary imbalances make economic cycles shorter and more abrupt, so the investor's mind and the holding period have to be adjusted accordingly.

---

[25] In the past 30 years, the IMF, Federal Reserve, ECB, and the Bank of Japan (BOJ) have missed their own estimates more than 80 percent of the time. Ned Davis explains in "Being Right or Making Money" (2000, Ned Davis Research) that international organizations' average hit in their expectations is 26 percent and, more importantly, that they have a historical upward bias, that is, they tend to err on the side of optimism, not for being prudent.

CHAPTER 2

Central Banks Don't Print Growth

"It's true, you can do anything you want to do"

—Phil Lynott

A liquidity trap is a situation when expansionary monetary policies, such as the increase in money supply, fail to stimulate economic growth because economic agents prefer to hold on to cash at any given rate, even with negative real interest rates. This happens because of the fear of more adverse events and the lack of attractive opportunities to deploy funds.

If there is a clear example of what a liquidity trap is, we can find it in the European Union.

Since the launch of QE in January 2015, until the end of 2016, the ECB has expanded its balance sheet by more than €2 trillion to reach 35 percent of the eurozone GDP.[1] While growth and inflation expectations have been revised down, the excess liquidity has soared to €1.1 trillion.

In terms of monetary aggregates, the increase in M3[2] was lower than 4 percent (annualized in 2016). Loans to the nonfinancial sectors grew a meager 2 percent.[3] All this with the greatest monetary stimulus seen since 2008.

What about inflation? It increased from 0.4 percent in September 2016 to 0.6 percent in December 2016. But this was fundamentally because of the cost of energy. Draghi himself recalled that "there are no convincing signs of recovery of underlying inflation" (January, 19 2017 ECB conference)—that which excludes energy and food.

---

[1] ECB official data.

[2] Broad money supply.

[3] Mario Draghi's statement on the eurozone economy December 2016.

The velocity of money (nominal GDP/M2)—which measures economic activity—is at multiyear lows and more liquidity and low rates do not help improve it.

Quantitative easing is disinflationary for prices because it sinks interest margins of banks by artificially lowering bond yields and makes economic agents behave with more caution—not rush to spend or to borrow—due to the perception that the cost and the quantity of money are artificial. But it is very inflationary in financial assets.

What these figures tell us is that growth is still very poor and the huge amount of monetary stimulus created from the central bank does not have the effect that its defenders promised. The ECB's balance sheet soared to €3.58 trillion, more than €400 billion above its 2012 high, and the accumulation of risks is more than evident, even if many decide to ignore them.

At the end of 2016, the ECB owns almost 10 percent of all the eurozone government bond market and 9 percent of the corporate debt, and that figure could double in one year.[4]

However, owning all those bonds has done nothing to improve economic conditions. Credit growth has remained subdued, broad money supply has stalled, which means that credit is not growing, and investment in the real economy has continued to decrease.[5]

As Fitch Ratings notes, investment in the economy in the eurozone remains 8 percent below 2007 levels and they cite "the crisis" as a reason but "pessimism about the medium-term growth outlook for the eurozone may also have played a part."[6] Fitch also notes that the outlook for business investment remained uncertain after two years of massive monetary stimulus. Investors polled in Fitch's annual senior investor survey stated they were "increasingly downbeat on companies' capital investment plans" and only 2 percent of those polled expected corporates to focus significantly on capex.[7]

---

[4] ECB, Reuters.

[5] Capex in the eurozone has fallen to 2007 levels according to Morgan Stanley and Deutsche Bank.

[6] Fitch Ratings, European Corporate Funding, October 2016.

[7] Fitch Ratings, European Investor Survey 2Q 2016.

As such, investors did not take more risk because liquidity was soaring and corporates did not invest more—because it was not needed. These economic agents decided to save more, to focus on strengthening the balance sheet and, in the case of investors, hoard negative-yielding bonds.

Why is it that families and companies do not decide to take on more debt and increase investment if rates are ultralow and liquidity is plentiful?

Because the central bank ignores the problem of overcapacity, which remains above 20 percent in the eurozone,[8] and the public perception that despite artificially low rates and manipulated money supply, economic conditions remain difficult. But also because the middle class suffers as real wages stall and labor market conditions become more uncertain. Therefore, solvent credit demand does not increase.

This is an important factor. It is not that the eurozone is not investing or that there is no demand for credit, rather the contrary—it simply is not as much as the central bank assumes it should be.

Why?

The central bank estimates that the rate of savings to investment is "too low" and therefore it must lower interest rates and help free the balance sheet of banks by purchasing their government bonds. However, the main problem is that the ratio of savings to investment is considered "low" only because the policy makers are comparing it to the bubble period[9]—the excessive accumulation of debt and poor allocation of capital from 2001 to 2007 that led to the crisis.[10] If one assumes a normalized credit decision process, we can perfectly understand that the deleveraging process of the real economy is not only healthy but also essential to avoid another crisis.

---

[8] Capacity utilization has been below 80 percent since the crisis, and low interest rates have actually perpetuated such overcapacity as nonperforming loans were refinanced.

[9] Even some rating agencies make their analysis comparing their data to that of 2007, when this year was the peak of excess.

[10] Private debt soared to 200 percent of GDP in many European countries, and family indebtedness doubled to 1.65 times the income of a household.

But all this would be fine if the liquidity trap would not simultaneously generate very negative consequences.

What Negative Consequences?

Government bond yields in the eurozone have fallen to all-time lows with the purchasing program of the ECB. The inflow of capital into risky assets soars[11] and risk premiums collapse, while financial asset valuations rise.[12]

As such, even if there is excess liquidity, yields are low, and the "risks" have been contained, the central bank cannot stop its purchase program or adjust it per the new reality because of the fear of a market crash. The central bank did not function as a transmission mechanism to improve the real economy, but as a perpetuator and instigator of yet another financial asset bubble.

The financial bubble is such that if the ECB decided to cut its purchase program to absorb the excess liquidity in the system, it could cause a market collapse because investors, who have been hoarding government bonds at unsustainably low rates and equities unsupported by fundamentals, would immediately trigger a sell-off.

If we make an analysis of the eurozone crisis, there was never a liquidity problem. The ECB had €120 billion in excess liquidity when the QE program was launched. Spain and other peripheral countries were already regaining strength and growing above the EU average. There was a problem of confidence in the survival of the eurozone and a large problem in the banking system, which at the peak of the crisis had total assets exceeding 320 percent of the eurozone GDP and nonperforming loans of more than €200 billion.[13]

These problems could have been contained with the same words— and no asset purchases—that Mario Draghi famously pronounced, "We

---

[11] Capital inflow into bonds led to more than €4.7 trillion of negative-yielding bonds in the eurozone in 2016.

[12] The Euro Stoxx 500 Price to Earnings ratio in 2016 is at almost 18x despite five consecutive years of zero earnings growth.

[13] European Banking Association.

will do whatever it takes and it will be enough,"[14] and with a series of targeted liquidity programs (TLTRO)[15] specifically designed to act as support for banks to reduce their imbalances and improve balance sheet while preventing the perverse incentive of perpetuating those same imbalances. A Europe-wide Troubled Asset Relief Program (TARP) program focused on return via dividends—a loan that has to be repaid and at the same time includes monitoring of actions—would have been equally effective without the liquidity trap risks. This system would have served as an effective tool to recover credit to SMEs and the real economy while providing effective penalties for the wrong use of the funds.

The ECB, I must say, has implemented its monetary policy because it was a clamor coming from the overindebted governments, not so much because the chairman and the committee believed liquidity measures were urgent. Proof of that is that asset classes and markets stabilized rapidly months before the ECB purchased a single bond, after the commitment to the euro was categorically affirmed by Mr. Draghi.

At least Mr. Draghi takes every available occasion to remind nations that they must implement structural reforms to make the central bank policy work. The ECB has also applied several measures to avoid excess risk-taking or incorrect use of funds, such as costs for holding unutilized liquidity and adding holdings of government bonds to increase margins through carry trades. But they are timid, and have not prevented the massive bubble.

Ask yourselves one question. Does anyone really believe that many peripheral European countries' government bond yields should be below the U.S. 10-year bond? Granted that some of those countries saw those bond yields soar to unjustified levels when doubts about the survival of the euro flooded the market, but since those fears were eradicated, bond yields in countries such as Portugal, Spain, and Italy have fallen to the lowest level on record because the ECB buys as much as it can from any issuance. In many cases, the ECB absorbed entire new issuances from sovereign bonds.

---

[14] July 26, 2012 at UK Trade & Investment's Global Investment Conference.
[15] Targeted Long-Term Refinancing Operations.

At the pace of purchases of government bonds seen in 2015 and 2016, the ECB would own the entire debt of the eurozone in 11 years.[16]

But This Is a Good Thing, Right?

If the central bank owns all the debt, governments will be able to spend freely without the constraints of market volatility and investor confidence. Think again. In 2017 alone, the eurozone needs to refinance €1.1 trillion of debt and, even with outstanding monetary stimulus, it has €125 billion of interest payments.[17] Japan, which we will discuss in a separate chapter, spends 22 percent of its budget in interest payments despite having close-to-zero interest rates for 19 years.

Deficit spending is not free even if central banks monetize all the debt. It has a very steep cost, via either economic stagnation, or stagflation.[18]

Draghi cannot be criticized for his work, which has been exemplary when it comes to highlighting challenges and risks. When he analyzed the eurozone's macroeconomic and monetary situation in 2016, he confirmed a very fragile environment and disappointing figures.

The European economy will grow by 1.7 percent each year in 2016 and 2017 and by 1.6 percent each year in 2018 and 2019. Despite flooding the system with liquidity, expectations have not increased. And we must note that the ECB has revised down its estimates of growth and inflation every year since 2011.

The Risks

The eurozone accumulates more than €4.2 trillion in bonds with zero or negative rates, according to Bloomberg.[19] See Figure 2.1.

The "inflation" that the media tells us does not exist, lies in the huge bubble of bonds and ultralow bond yields. This accumulation of risk is

---

[16] Assuming €80 billion of purchases per month and the eurozone maintaining its net refinancing needs.

[17] Bloomberg.

[18] Weak growth with significantly higher inflation.

[19] December 2016.

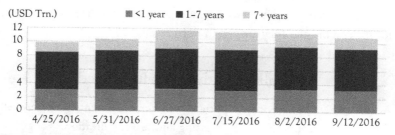

Figure 2.1 Negative-yielding bonds worldwide

Source: Fitch Ratings, Bloomberg.

exactly as dangerous as that between 2006 and 2008 but potentially more difficult to contain. This is because economic agents—particularly governments, which are much more indebted—are not in a better position of solvency and repayment capacity today than they were in that period. This leads to inefficient and heavily indebted governments falling into the trap of thinking that cheap money will always exist and deciding to increase their imbalances, which adds to deficits and increases the risk of a debt shock when rates rise.

If EU countries get used to ultralow rates, the risk of multibillion nominal and real losses in bond portfolios and pension funds is enormous, because the tiniest tilt in inflation will make the house of cards collapse. Goldman Sachs estimates losses of $2.5 trillion worldwide from a 1 percent rise in inflation.[20] It is so relevant that if interest rates raised a stunted 1 percent in the European Union, it would lead to massive budget cuts to maintain current deficits.

Of course, Draghi does not stop repeating that this period of excessive liquidity must serve to correct imbalances and implement structural reforms. But no one seems to listen. Cheap money calls for cheap action. More "fiscal stimulus" and more spending.

The problem is that the structural challenges of the European economy—demography and overcapacity—are not solved by perpetuating imbalances, because governments and economic agents simply get used to seemingly temporary measures as if they were eternal.

---

[20] Goldman Sachs, Implications of Rising Inflation Expectations on Bonds, December 2016.

What is troubling is that most European countries are not prepared for the end of QE. They are geared to its extension.

The Fallacy of the "Wealth Effect"

At this stage, I believe it is important to make a differentiation between the placebo effect of quantitative easing and real stabilization.

In 2012, Reuters's Pedro Costa asked Ben Bernanke, chairman of the Federal Reserve, the following question:

> *Speaking to people on the sidelines of the Jackson Hole conference, the concern about the remarks that you made is that they could clearly see the effect on rates and they could see the effect on the stock market, but they couldn't see how that had helped the economy. So, I think there's a fear that, over time, this has been a policy that's helping Wall Street but not doing that much for Main Street. So, could you describe, in some detail, how does it really differ from trickle-down economics?*[21]

The answer is revealing:

> *This is a Main Street policy, because what we're about here is trying to get jobs going. We are trying to create more employment, we are trying to meet our maximum employment mandate, so that's the objective. The tools we have involve affecting financial asset prices, and those are the tools of monetary policy. There are a number of different channels— mortgage rates, interest rates, corporate bond rates, but also the prices of various assets, like, for example, the prices of homes. To the extent that home prices begin to rise, consumers will feel wealthier; they'll feel more disposed to spend. If house prices are rising, people may be more willing to buy homes because they think that they'll make a better return on that purchase. So house prices is one vehicle. Stock prices—many people own stocks directly or indirectly. The issue here is whether or not improving asset prices generally will make people more willing to spend. One of the main concerns that firms have is there is not enough demand, there's not*

---

[21] September 13, 2012 Transcript of Chairman Bernanke's Press Conference.

*enough people coming and demanding their products. And if people feel
that their financial situation is better because their 401(k) looks better
or, for whatever reason, their house is worth more, they are more willing
to go out and spend, and that's going to provide the demand that firms
need in order to be willing to hire and to invest.*

· This looks interesting, but it does not work.

Financial repression inflates the price of financial assets but at the
same time destroys the purchasing power of the currency, and devalues
the wealth accumulated in deposits.[22]

Over 81 percent of stock wealth is held by the top 10 percent of the
population. In fact, over 80 percent of U.S. citizens have 9.9 percent
or less of their wealth in stocks.[23] (In the European Union or in Japan
it is even lower.)[24] That same overwhelming majority of U.S. citizens
have most of their wealth in deposits, which got completely obliterated
with the policy of devaluing the currency.[25] Meanwhile, real salaries
decline[26] and the ability of the middle class to pay debts and mortgages
shrinks.

At the same time, rising house prices do not create a "wealth effect"
to borrowers with a mortgage, and they certainly make it more difficult
for nonowners to get into the so-called property ladder. It is no surprise
that throughout the housing recovery in the United States the number
of homes bought without any mortgage rose dramatically.[27] Quantitative

---

[22] Ultra-Easy Monetary Policy and the Law of Unintended Consequences.
William White. Working Paper no 126. Federal Reserve Bank of Dallas, Globalization and Monetary Policy Institute.

[23] Gallup.

[24] Less than 6 to 7 percent according to Eurostat and the BOJ.

[25] The dollar devalued more than 33 percent against its currency basket throughout QE (www.forbes.com/sites/charleskadlec/2012/02/06/the-federal-reserves-
explicit-goal-devalue-the-dollar-33/#5d13cbbb7865).

[26] Real salaries in the United States fell throughout QE and by 2016 have not
recovered to 2008 levels. Meanwhile labor participation rate fell to the lowest
since 1978 with more than 11 million workers leaving the labor force.

[27] www.doctorhousingbubble.com/americans-that-own-home-with-no-mort-
gage-free-and-clear/

easing benefits most those who have access to the rising financial assets and to leverage. That is, the super-rich. It is no surprise that the left media complains about rising inequality. Quantitative easing is basically supporting the wealthier at the expense of the savers. The problem with the media is that they see inequality and demand even more so-called "expansionary" measures as the solution.

The idea that rising stock markets, lower bond yields, and higher house prices benefit main street is simply ridiculous. And the rise of populist alternatives like Bernie Sanders and the victory of Donald Trump in the 2016 elections are further proof that the "economic miracle" simply did not reach the middle classes.

At least trickle-down economics[28] has some merit and reality to it. During the Thatcher mandate in the United Kingdom, real income per capita rose by over 34 percent, including for the poorest segments—this, with two recessions, a war, and 11 percent unemployment. Thatcher lowered taxes (from the top marginal rate of 83 percent to 40 percent) but kept tax revenues at 40 percent of GDP. Under Reagan real per capita disposable income increased by 18 percent from 1982 to 1989, meaning the American standard of living increased by almost 20 percent in just seven years. The poverty rate declined every year from 1984 to 1989, dropping by one-sixth from its peak.[29]

Good idea. Instead of printing money so that governments and speculators get wealthier, let us create money for "the people."

The Disaster of "People's QE" and Modern Monetary Theory (MMT)

"Money is the general medium of exchange, the thing that all other goods and services are traded for, the final payment for such goods and services in the market"

—Murray N. Rothbard

---

[28] Lowering taxes, cutting public spending, and letting real disposable income rise.

[29] Peter Ferrara, Reaganomics vs. Obamanomics. Facts and Figures. Forbes. May 5, 2011.

The apparent failure of expansive monetary policies created a "new" school. I say *new* with irony because it is the oldest school in history, to create money out of nothing to finance "the people." And "the people" being, of course, the government.

It is called the modern monetary theory but it is just the same thing that has been done many times in history from the French Assignats, to the policies of Allende in Chile,[30] Kicillof in Argentina,[31] or Maduro in Venezuela.[32] And with the same results—massive inflation, destruction of currencies, then blaming "speculators" for the stagflation, and finally, bankruptcy.

Because there is nothing "social" about mass inflationary policies. From Allende to Kirchner and Maduro, printing and inflating is not a social policy; it is theft.

The indiscriminate creation of money not supported by savings is always behind the greatest crises, and there is always someone willing to justify it as both a problem and its solution.

We must understand what money is and why "creating it" artificially without support destroys more than it apparently improves.

Money is a means of exchange and payment that must be widely accepted. If citizens lose confidence in its value due to manipulation, it disappears as a means of exchange, a store of value, and unit of account. That confidence is not dictated by a committee or a government by decree.

Money in its function as a means of exchange facilitates trade, preventing barter. When its value is questioned, when it loses its place as a reserve, the economy is destroyed, going from crisis to crisis, which are becoming faster and more violent.[33]

---

[30] The HyperInflation of Chile: Lessons for Us All, Economic Policy Journal, 2010.

[31] Argentina: Close To Default…Again www.dlacalle.com/argentina-close-to-default-again/

[32] Venezuela entered hyperinflation in 2016. It is only the seventh country in the history of Latin America to have that dubious distinction. Technically, hyperinflation occurs when month-on-month inflation tops 50 percent for 30 days straight.

[33] Loss of Confidence and Currency Crises. Willy Spanjers. Economics Discussion Papers from School of Economics. June 1998.

There are very evident examples of currency crisis generated by reckless increase in money supply with no respect for the warning signs of inflation and devaluation. Maduro's Venezuela (Figure 2.3), Zimbabwe (see Figure 2.2), Kirchner's Argentina, the Assignats disaster in the French revolution, the Weimar Republic—all those examples generated mass

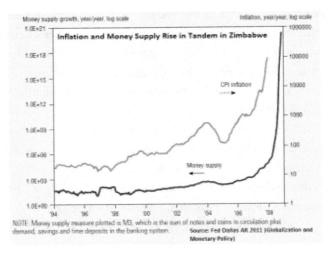

Figures 2.2 Evidence of the impact of reckless money printing on inflation

Source: Dallas Fed, IMF.

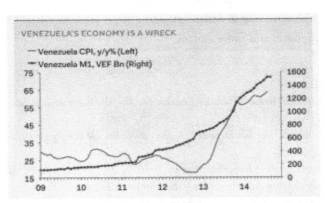

Figure 2.3 Evidence of the impact of reckless money printing on inflation

Source: Dallas Fed, IMF.

poverty, scarcity, out of control inflation, and widespread loss of confidence in the currency.

Inflation is always a monetary effect. It is the symptom of a clear imbalance.

Money Versus Inflation

Money, when created from the expansion of artificial credit is also destroyed—a serious financial crisis, defaults, falling real assets—based on unjustified expectations.

Whether that artificial money creation is through credit to governments, people, or companies, the outcome is the same. The distortion generated by inefficient allocation of capital has the same effect.

Modern monetary policy advocates using the expansion of the central banks' balance sheet for helicopter money, that is, to give newly created money directly to the people—and for financing government spending. It is the same mistake as QE but it shifts the imbalance from financial markets to the average citizen.

It sounds promising. The central bank "creates" new money and gives it to every citizen, so they can spend. This boosts consumption and improves the economy. Except, it doesn't. The currency devalues and imports, goods, and services become more expensive. The economy does not receive the boost that the media and inflationist economists estimate because the negative effect of rising prices lowers the assumed impact on consumption and also because some citizens will decide to save that money. Even in contained environments like the cities in Europe that have created local currencies to boost regional consumption, there is no evidence of any improvement in either the economy or its ability to endure crises.[34]

Consider the example of Argentina, which has seen an inflation of 350 percent since 2008 from what the government called an "inclusive"

---

[34] Greek citizens who accepted the local system called TEM (in Volos, Greece) in 2010 have not seen any improvement in the economy or benefited relative to the rest of the country. The same is true for Bristol, UK.

policy of creating money to pay "employment and public investment," increasing money supply by 30 percent per year.

But the desire to think that making money out of nothing "creates wealth" and has no consequences is simply a pseudo-religious prejudice, not a reality. Any analysis of the creation of money and inflation shows that the effect is evident and that it always ends with a financial crisis, higher inflation, and greater unemployment. The "placebo effect," the illusion of growth that is created shortterm, erupts with a major crisis in a short period of time.

What the socialist inflationists of the MMT school forget is the effect of saturation of debt and the impact of the continuous creation of money on money velocity, which measures the economic activity.

Creating money to subsidize hypertrophied states or to perpetuate the misallocation of capital of private agents are the same. An additional unit of indebtedness does not generate enough nominal GDP growth to reduce debt accumulation, even if the stock is monetized; it fuels the next shock with greater virulence.

The relationship between money creation and inflation since 1960 is direct as can be seen in "Inflation versus M2 Money Supply from 1960."[35] See Figure 2.4 with more recent data.

The saturation effect and the manipulation of capital allocation in the economy favoring specific sectors designated by the government plunge economic activity, as financial repression and the tax burden on families and companies increase. Input costs soar, tax burden increases, expansion cycles are shorter, and margins are weaker.

But the theory is based on the idea that if "the government spends, economic activity increases and there is a multiplier effect." Public spending multiplier has been proven to be inexistent, even negative, in many studies. In the experience of more than 44 countries it is shown that the multiplier effect is nonexistent in open and highly indebted economies.[36]

---

[35] Consumer Inflation vs. Money Supply Growth 1960 to 2016 William G. Dewald, St Louis Fed.

[36] Ethan Ilzetzki, Enrique Mendoza, and Carlos Végh, "How Big (Small?) are Fiscal Mutlipliers?"

Figure 2.4 International data on inflation and money growth (N. Gregory Mankiw)

The accumulated deficit means higher taxes later. Consumer preferences, given financial repression, do not improve because the government spends. Government spending only generates more overcapacity and consumers spend less knowing taxes will rise. The new monetarists forget that their recommendation is precisely what led Brazil and China to industrial overcapacity of 27 percent and 38 percent respectively.[37] And these are not populations with demographic problems.

Growth is not poor due to lack of public spending, which, globally, is at its highest in 50 years. It is poor because of the attack on the consumer through taxes[38] to pay for said expense and the assault on the saver through financial repression by means of devaluation and lowering of rates.

Other examples of the disaster that "creating money for the people" were seen in Chile with Allende, Zimbabwe, and Venezuela. The perpetrators of this disaster always call it "economic warfare"—accusing businessmen or speculators of the consequences of monetary irresponsibility.

---

[37] 2016.

[38] OECD tax burden reached a historical record level in 2016.

To flood the public sector with "new" money without any sterilization,[39] monetizing everything, which is called "Popular QE," is the same madness and has the same effects.

It assumes that the central bank loses its already-questioned independence and directly becomes a government agency that prints money when the government wants, but that increase of money supply does not become part of the transmission mechanism that reaches all parts of the economy; the new money is only for the government to finance a "Public Investment Bank."

The mistake of the socialist monetarists of the popular QE is that their theory starts from the correct argument that monetary expansion as we know it today does not work. However, instead of understanding that printing currency is simply an unjust transfer of wealth from savers to the inefficient and the indebted, they do not see monetary expansion as the problem, but the distribution mechanism. So, they want to avoid any transmission mechanism and create money directly for governments.

The first problem is obvious. The central bank would create money without any backing, which is the equivalent of a bank lending without any assets. And that money would be used for white elephants—massive public spend projects without any evident economic return because if there was one it would have been invested in the past. The public investment bank would provide unlimited funding, generating elevated risks of irresponsibility in spending. And it is an obvious displacement of incentives to waste money. But it would also generate disproportionate negative effects on the private sector as unfair competition would mean that the only sectors that would survive would be the ones attached to governments (what we know as cronyism).

The second problem is that this public bank's mounting nonperforming loans from lending to projects without profitability will be covered with taxes to citizens and the private sector.

The third problem is that inflation created by these projects is a burden on the disposable income and purchasing power of the citizen who does not benefit from this expansion of "unlimited" spending. Taxes

---

[39] Sterilization: selling to the open market some of the bonds purchased by the central bank.

rise, cost of living soars and, above all, a large part of the business fabric gets destroyed, because the government has unlimited privileged credit. To think that this inflation leads to higher salaries is a fallacy that is demonstrated by history. It has always proven that real wages fall to historic lows.

This policy, as we have said, has been implemented many times in the past, and every time with disastrous consequences. It is the model that sank the French revolution with the Assignats[40] and the Argentina of Cristina Fernández de Kirchner and her minister Axel Kicillof.[41] It is a model that has only created massive inflation and recession, or, stagflation.

To think that the government can decide the amount of money it needs and spend it on what it wants without dramatic negative consequences is simply science fiction.

Aristocrats of public spending, who have never created a company or hired anyone with their savings and effort, always think that intervening in the creation of money and in the economy will save everything.

Do they know? Of course, they do. They do not care, because for them the State is infallible and the objective of political dominance of the economy excuses every other mistake. "Socialism has a history of failures so brutal that only a group of pseudo-intellectuals can ignore it and say that they will make it different."[42]

Increasing money supply more than the historical growth of nominal GDP always creates huge imbalances that lead to a great crisis.

The MMT is not new. It is the same old search for unlimited economic government control at all costs financed at the expense of all others.

Ecuador Avoids Depression by Not Printing Money

Gabriela Calderón de Burgos explained how Ecuador, unable to print "money for the people," avoided depression by having its currency pegged

---

[40] Revolutionary France's Road to Hyperinflation, Frank Hollenbeck, 2013.
[41] A massive annual inflation of 40 percent and currency controls, printing money.
[42] Thomas Sowell.

to the U.S. dollar, and, in turn, escaped the monstrous inflation and monetary disaster of Venezuela and Argentina.[43]

Government officials repeated that they had managed the economic recession even being tied up for not having their own currency.

What would have happened if, from the beginning of the problems in 2014, instead of having been dollarized Ecuador would have had a national currency and followed the monetary policy of its ideological partners Venezuela and Argentina?

Politicians would have tried to combat the economic cycle, spending more, printing money while foreign currency inflows collapsed, and trying to monetize the expense, leading to a massive depreciation of the currency.

The Ecuadorians would have reacted by rejecting such a currency that loses value every day, as Argentinians and Venezuelan citizens have, in search of another that maintains value. This would have led, like in the countries mentioned, to massive withdrawals of the Sucre—the Ecuadorian currency—from banks to buy U.S. dollars, gold, or any other value reserve option.

This is not counterfactual. It happened in the late 1990s, when the Central Bank of Ecuador (BCE), seeing the fall of the Sucre against the dollar, intervened in the foreign exchange market to try to stop its decline, spending all its foreign currency reserve in the process and fuelling depression and massive inflation.

Seeing reserves fall, people become even more nervous and withdrawals accelerate. When this happened in Ecuador, the central bank sought to curb capital flight and withdrawals of deposits by raising the interest rate. It did not stop the stagflation process.

How much did they issue? In 1996 money supply registered an annual increase of 51.2 percent; in 1997 it was 28.2 percent; in 1998, 38.6 percent; and in 1999, 149 percent. Along with this orgy of money creation came the galloping inflation, which went from 24 percent in 1996 to 52 percent in 1999 and to 96 percent in 2000.

---

[43] El Instituto Independiente, January 2017.

It should be noted that the huge increase in money supply created such a depreciation of the currency that it triggered a bank run and massive capital flights. The central bank lent the banks so they could pay their customers, who desperately wanted to convert their Sucres to dollars. The currency, economic, and financial crises were halted in January 2000 when dollarization was adopted.

From 2014, when the government budget reached its peak and the fall in oil prices began, Ecuador's funding gap rose considerably. Spending cuts ensued but they were not enough, avoiding inevitable and deeper structural adjustments.

In its stubbornness, the Ecuador government replaced high oil revenues with an aggressive increase in public debt at high rates. Money is never enough, and it is easy to assume that if, for example, during 2015 to 2017 the Ecuador government had counted with its own currency, much of the financing gap would have been covered by a significant increase in money issuance and a spiral of aggravating phenomena similar to or worse than the ones seen in 1999.

Despite the increase in debt, which stands at 33 percent of GDP, still below that of other countries in the area, dollarization has allowed Ecuador to pass the rout of oil prices with moderate inflation and much less economic pain than faced by Venezuela or Argentina, and without destroying the country's finances. Far from complaining about dollarization, government officials should recognize that it was the best economic reform introduced in the country.[44]

What Next?

Monetary and fiscal stimuli have been implemented with the objectives of spurring growth and reducing imbalances caused in the previous crisis, and to help reduce debt.

However, at the end of 2016 global debt exceeds $217 trillion or 327 percent of GDP, and in the first nine months of 2016, global debt increased by $11 trillion, $5.3 trillion of which was from governments.

[44] Gabriela Calderón writes for El Cato and El Universo.

Global debt has increased by more than $67 trillion in the eight years of the stimulus and deficit spending bonanza.[45]

The monetary laughing gas machine has not delivered, and its consequences are felt all over the world, as seen in emerging markets: currencies collapsing, commodities at multiyear lows, stagflation, and so on. Years of cheap dollars flooding the markets and long-term investments financed with short-term, QE-driven liquidity created overcapacity, distortions, and bubbles bursting in slow motion in front of our eyes ahead of a rate hike of … 0.25 percentage points!

One of the biggest difficulties that the OECD faces is that it has launched massive stimulus plans that have ballooned the balance sheets of central banks, and price inflation has not been created, while growth remains more than disappointing. This is what I call the three Ls: "low interest rates, low growth, low inflation."

In the stimulus period the G7 countries alone have added almost $18 trillion in debt to a record $140 trillion, with nearly $5 trillion from the expansion of the balance sheets of their central banks, to produce only $1 trillion of nominal GDP. That is, in five years, to generate $1 of growth the G7 have "spent" $18, with 30 percent coming from central banks.[46]

To try to tackle the "crisis," the central bank prints money—expands credit—to buy bonds from the financial system and private sectors in order to "alleviate" the balance sheet of the banks and help credit flow to the real economy.

However, by perpetuating this, the central bank has made the mistake of becoming the largest single purchaser, thus sustaining "bubble" valuations.

First mistake: The central bank buys bonds with a valuation that is significantly higher to fundamentals. Therefore, although these asset purchases generate a return—the central bank receives coupons of those bonds—the market price of the principal is justified only by the fact that the central bank buys most of the supply.

Imagine you have a market and one single buyer acquires all the products irrespective of demand. Prices go through the roof because this

---

[45] Institute of International Finance (IIF). Global Debt Monitor—January 2017.
[46] Deutsche Bank, Torsten Slok, IMF data.

"superbuyer" inflates them. Then, when it stops acquiring those products, what happens in the market? Exactly! Prices fall too aggressively. So the superbuyer needs to keep buying to avoid a massive collapse in prices that he himself inflated.

Second mistake: thinking that the previous valuation was unjustified. By extending monetary policy and asset buybacks for years the central bank goes from buying "bargains" that actually traded at an unjustified discount, to purchase "whatever" is available. And it generates a bubble in bonds. It creates its own trap as the possible capital loss of buying overvalued assets is "fixed" by the central bank itself, fuelling the bubble.

Third mistake: The risk curve shifts and markets increasingly pay less yield for greater risk. Thus, each new program of monetary expansion generates two perverse effects: Banks and investors still prefer bonds and liquid assets, and invest less in the real economy; and, the central bank is forced to perpetuate the asset purchase program in order to avoid another financial crisis. That is why money velocity collapses.

After all, excessive risk-taking, be it by the financial sector or by the central bank, is the same. The imbalances that are generated are similar. However, if the financial system creates an asset bubble, it is spread among a large number of entities with different risk exposures. If the central bank feeds the bubble, especially in sovereign bonds, it creates more financial repression, printing more for longer at the expense of taxpayers and savers, whether through a lower value of the currency, more inflation, or through higher taxes.

That is why the words of Mario Draghi are so important: "Monetary policy cannot replace reforms. It is crucial to have cooperation between economic policy and structural reforms."[47]

Central banks cannot print growth. They may buy some time, but the effect, like monetary laughing gas, is short-lived.

One of the most dangerous statements we usually hear is that "fundamentals have not changed." They have—a lot.

If we analyze the global growth expectations of international organizations, the first thing that should concern us is the speed and intensity

---

[47] ECB minutes, 2016.

of downward revisions. In the United States, for example, we had an expectation of growth of 3.5 percent revised to 2 percent in less than six months in 2015. If we looked at the revision of the estimates for the fourth quarter of 2015 of the major economies of the world, they were downgraded by 40 percent in less than 20 days.[48]

Not surprisingly, the IMF and the OECD cut their expectations almost every three months. Can they be wrong? Yes, but if we look at history, they have mostly been optimistic, not cautious.

This downgrade process is not over.

China is one of the key reasons. The global economy has geared itself to justify huge investments to serve the expected Chinese growth, ignoring its fragility. China, with an overcapacity of nearly 60 percent and total debt already exceeding 250 percent of GDP,[49] has a financial problem that will be dealt only with large devaluations and lower growth. That landing will not be short. An excess of more than a decade is not resolved in a year. This exports disinflation to the world, as China devalues and tries to export more, and when the "engine of the world" slows down because it ends an unsustainable model, the world is left with the excess in global installed capacity created for that growth mirage. Commodities fall and mining- and energy-dependent countries suffer.

Consensus economists have consistently overestimated the positive effects of monetary policy and expansionary fiscal measures, and ignored the risks. Emergency measures have become perpetual, and the global economy, after years of expansionary policies shows three signs which increase fragility.

Excess liquidity and low interest rates have led to increase in total debt by more than $67 trillion, led by growth in public debt of 9 percent per annum, according to the World Bank.[50]

Second, industrial overcapacity has been perpetuated by the refinancing of inefficient and indebted sectors. Governments do not understand

---

[48] Average annual downgrade of IMF and OEC estimates since 2001 is 20 percent from January to October, according to Bloomberg.

[49] Total debt, December 2016.

[50] World Bank 2016 Review.

the cumulative effect of this overcapacity because they always attribute it to lack of demand, not misallocation of capital.

In 2008, there was an overcapacity problem mainly in developed countries. With the huge expansion plans in emerging markets, overcapacity has accumulated and has been transferred to two-thirds of the global economy. Brazil, China, the OPEC countries, and Southeast Asia join the developed nations in suffering the consequences of investment in huge white elephant projects of questionable profitability "to boost GDP."

Financial repression has not led to the acceleration of activity from economic agents. Currency wars and manipulation of the amount and price of money make the velocity of money slow down. Because the perception of risk is higher, and solvent credit does not grow, as the average cost of capital[51] is still greater than expected returns, causing debt repayment capacity to shrink despite lower rates, according to Fitch and Moody's.

A balance-sheet recession is not solved with more liquidity and incentives to borrow. And it will not be solved with large infrastructure spending and wider deficits spending.

Offsetting the slowdown from China and emerging markets with public spending is fiscally impossible.

Most economies have exceeded the threshold of debt saturation, when an additional unit of debt does not generate a nominal GDP increase.

The global need for infrastructure and education is about $855 billion annually, per the World Bank.[52] All that extra expense, if carried out, does not make up for even half of the impact of China slowing down to a sustainable growth level, even if we assume fiscal multipliers that are more than discredited by reality.[53]

---

[51] Convertibility, currency controls and cots of capital, 1950–1999. Hans-Joachim Voth.

[52] World Bank estimates of investment requirements, 2015.

[53] Ethan Ilzetzki, Enrique Mendoza, Carlos Végh, "How Big (Small?) are Fiscal Mutlipliers?" http://users.nber.org/~confer/2011/SI2011/IFM/Ilzetzki_Mendoza_Vegh.pdf

China's share in global GDP is about 16 percent;[54] its slowdown to sustainable growth cannot be compensated with white elephants elsewhere. This is not pessimism; it is mathematics.

Monetary laughing gas only buys time and gives the illusion of growth, but ignores the imbalances it generates. Financial repression encourages reckless short-term borrowing, attacks disposable income, and is accompanied by tax increases that affect consumption.

The capital misallocation created by excess liquidity and zero rates has led to a credit bubble in high-yield and sovereign bonds, masking their true ability to repay. Looking at the figure globally, maturities of corporate and sovereign bonds to 2020 are nearly $20 trillion. Up to 14 percent of those are considered "nonperforming."[55]

With all these elements of fragility, it is normal to assume we face an environment of low growth, but there are reasons to doubt a global recession.

The Chinese problem is mostly in local currency and within its financial sector, reducing the risk of contagion to the global financial system.

Dollar reserves in emerging countries only fell modestly and remain at record levels after a 50 percent collapse in commodity prices.

Although default risks in emerging markets, mining, and commodities rose, the combined total failed to reach a fraction of the extent of the real estate bubble risk in 2008.

Consumption continues to increase due to the growth in the global middle class and the effect of technology, which provides efficiency and good disinflation.

This is a slowdown from oversupply, not a credit crunch led by financial risk, and as such it puts in question the possibility of a global recession. But increased consumption will not compensate for the saturation of the obsolete indebted industrial growth model.

The global economy faces a long period of weak growth, but we should not confuse it with a global recession. Repeating the mistakes of the past will not change the landscape—it will perpetuate it.

---

[54] 2016.

[55] Standard and Poor's.

Negative real rates will not stimulate investment. They slow lending to the real economy and encourage short-term speculation.

The exit from a balance-sheet recession is not going to come from the same mistake of increasing public spending and adding debt. It will only be solved when increasing disposable income of households, not attack it with financial repression, becomes the main policy objective.

But this is the great mistake—to think that, because "nothing has happened" so far, it will not happen again. Economist Alan Taylor shows how credit booms lead to both financial crises and longer and deeper recessions than normal.[56] Financial crises were common in the nineteenth and early twentieth centuries, happening about every 15 to 20 years, and following the end of the Bretton Woods System, the world has seen twice the number of financial crises, although—and this is important—they have become more frequent and less severe.[57] So, yes, the reader does not have to be a rocket scientist or a top economist to predict that, at some point in the next five years, there will be a major financial crisis. The difficulty is to predict *when*.

Bubbles are not difficult to see. The challenge is to understand when they will be pricked.

The main lesson from this chapter is that monetary policy may have some effect when panic and contagion risk are unjustified, like in the breakup of the euro, but can soon become a trap by providing perverse incentives to prolong imbalances.

The fact that those perverse incentives exist with the transmission mechanism of commercial banks does not make the same policy without such mechanism any more effective. It creates different, and equally dangerous, negative incentives.

For investors, the main lesson from the European experience with QE is that "Buy the Dip" mentality does not work if fundamentals don't improve.

---

[56] Alan M. Taylor, "Credit, Financial Stability, and the Macroeconomy," Annual Review of Economics. 2015.

[57] Michael Bordo, Barry Eichengreen, Daniela Klingebiel, Maria Soledad Martinez-Periaand, Andrew K. Rose, "Is the crisis problem growing more severe," Economic Policy, Vol. 16. 2001.

The European QE experience yielded strong returns for bond investors but resulted in a value trap for equity investors. The main reason was that, while in the United States financial repression was used by companies to boost share buybacks and dividends, and banks rapidly strengthened to return the loans received and escape from intervention, in Europe companies simply continued to act as if nothing had happened and banks fell into the trap of QE thinking it would be positive for earnings. And it wasn't.

CHAPTER 3

Debt Is Not an Asset.
The Relative Success of
the U.S. QE

"I will choose a path that's clear, I will choose free will"

—Neil Peart

One thing we must understand by now is that, if governments benefit from financial repression, it will both continue and have commentators that defend it.

As such, we must understand how cycles function and behave, rigorously understanding what parts of the economy are going well and what is behaving poorly. This is especially important because we can be right at analyzing the risks and forget there are elements that have worked.

There are parts of the economy that have benefitted from low rates and high liquidity, but when the result is $9 trillion of added debt for a disappointing $3.6 trillion of GDP growth in eight years, it shows the fragility of the benefits and the risk of the accumulated imbalances.

But there are commentators that see differently; some even think that the national debt is not a risk, but an asset.

Is Debt Really an Asset?

At the end of the day, some economists will say that the government deficit is just money created that goes to the economy and creates more growth and wealth for citizens, and the government never has to repay such debt. It just issues promissory notes that are never repaid, just refinanced, with an interest. Therefore, the government debt is in fact an asset.

That's essentially the situation with the U.S. national "debt." The United States issues money by deficit spending. It puts more money into private accounts than it takes out via taxes. The private sector has more balance-sheet assets (but no more liabilities, so it has more "net worth," the balancing item on the right-hand side of its balance sheet). The treasury has made no promises to redeem that new money for ... anything (except maybe ... different government-issued assets). It's just out there.[1]

Is it not great? More like magic.

Except, it is not true.

The deficit spending and debt created exceed the total goods and services of the economy—in the case of the United States, by more than 100 percent.

Total debt in the economy is also higher than the sum of savings, goods, and services, in the United States, by 300 percent.[2]

Even if none of the public debt is repaid, it still costs an outstanding amount of money in interests every year.[3]

Furthermore, by continuing to issue more money, the purchasing power of the currency erodes, and real wealth is not created, but destroyed.

And as the government enters the spiral of solving the imbalances with more currency issuances and further deficits, the economy enters as well into the vicious circle of unproductive debt and secular stagnation.

If creating money out of thin air generated wealth, Venezuela, Zimbabwe, and Argentina would be the richest countries in the world.

The reason why the United States can conduct its expansive monetary policy is precisely because the U.S. dollar continues to be a reserve of value and the entire world trusts that the government will actually repay those debts with more than just inflation. Furthermore, it is the promise and commitment to control the rise in deficits and to end that policy which keeps the U.S. dollar as a reserve of value. Breaking the trust that the entire world concedes to the U.S. economy by breaking the promise

---

[1] http://evonomics.com/isnt-time-stop-calling-national-debt/
[2] Private and Public Debt.
[3] www.treasurydirect.gov/govt/reports/ir/ir_expense.htm

of payment and forgetting the importance of a secondary market, where sterilization of part of that debt issued is an integral part of such confidence, would destroy the perceived value of the currency for the rest of the world.

A currency is only worth something because most of the population accepts that perceived value.

Therefore, no, debt is not an asset. Even Marx considered it fictitious capital.[4] If it were an asset, a government would be able to deficit-spend as much as it liked and whenever it wanted, and there would be no consequences. And there are. To disregard the numerous financial crises generated by the accumulation of debt as anomalies and promote perpetual imbalances is not only reckless, but suicidal.

Making Financial Repression a Market Trade

So far, we have talked about impacts on the real economy and put forward the risks created in a ballooning financial bubble.

The first QE program in the United States showcased just that. The theory supporting financial repression is that if bonds and financial assets are made increasingly unattractive with lower yield, and cash becomes unappealing due to the ongoing process of devaluation and lower rates, investors will channel the excess liquidity and savings to the real economy, consuming more and boosting capital expenditure.

However, capital expenditure in nonfinancial sectors collapsed to the lowest levels in real terms after an all-too-brief period of exuberance. Quantitative easing was launched in 2009, and, by 2012, capital expenditure growth was stalling, then falling, every year until 2016.[5]

Instead of funneling funds and incentivizing the real economy, the expansionary policy has been inflating financial markets' expectations and generating excess in equity and bond markets. See Figure 3.1.

There was a certain merit to the idea. Trying to stimulate demand in a moment of absolute panic when markets and liquidity had simply dried up was reasonable, but failing to understand that the same

---

[4] Capital III (Moscow: Foreign Languages Publishing House, 1958).

[5] Standard & Poor's Global Corporate Capital Expenditure Survey 2016.

Figure 3.1 Federal reserve balance sheet vs. S&P 500 index

Source: Bloomberg, Jeroen Blokland.

policy—massively lowering rates—was behind the bubble that led to the crisis and ultimately to said panic meant that all other considerations were forgotten.

The fact that the Federal Reserve took the economic data at face value and accepted a level of unemployment that was falling as millions left the workforce showed how easily the shift went from stopping panic to focusing too much on the behavior of markets.

Questions started to arise all over the world when two things happened: policy shifted from stabilizing markets to supporting the rising valuations, and at the same time, the carefully designed estimates of growth for the years ahead—the infamous hockey sticks—were consistently missed.

So, in essence, two things happened.

Investors started to behave against the macro data. The consensual trade was to buy the weakening economic data in the hope that it would force the central banks to increase and intensify the expansionary policies. Markets had realized that monetary policy inflated asset prices and therefore celebrated when job claims rose, when growth estimates were revised down, and when companies published poor results. "Buy the Dip" became the norm.

Investors did not undertake a great rotation out of bonds into equities and out of equities into capital investments.

Investors simply accumulated more and more exposure to short-term liquid assets.

Capital expenditure, as mentioned before, rose only for a short period of time boosted by Oil and Gas and mining, as commodities—denominated in U.S. dollars—saw a massive increase in price as the U.S. currency devalued.

The Commodity Research Bureau (CRB) commodity index rose almost 100 percent, but neither supply and demand metrics nor global economic growth supported such a rise above 2008 peaks. This created an illusion of wealth for commodity producers that led many emerging markets to adapt to an extraordinary increase in dollar revenues that were used to finance long-term projects in local currency, which planted the seed for what became the next emerging-market crisis. We will explore in detail what the "sudden stop" means in the next chapter.

Markets expecting a "melt-up"[6] based on poor economic data was one of the clearest perverse incentives of stimulus.

A 2015 report from the Bank of America pointed out the perverse effects of QE and monetary stimulus.[7] After more than 600 rate cuts and excess of $12 trillion of money supply expansion in the period analyzed:

- For every job created in the United States in the years of QE, companies bought back $296,000 in shares.
- $100 invested in the stock market would be worth $205 while real wages stayed below 2008 levels.

The zero interest rate policy and asset purchase programs of central banks have proven to be more favorable to risky assets and unicorns than to workers, savers, companies, and the labor market.

Monetary stimulus was launched to improve macroeconomic data and market sentiment.

As such, asset valuations ballooned on the hope of recovery.

---

[6] http://articles.orlandosentinel.com/2012-09-08/news/ct-biz-0909-gail-20120908_1_twitter-gailmarksjarvis-stimulus-expectations-stock-market

[7] Bank of America Merrill Lynch, 2015. Michael Hartnett. November, 2015.

Once that economic situation proved to be less benign, markets acquired more short-term liquid assets in the anticipation that new easing would happen.

This created as well a level of valuation in those financial assets that was self-perpetuated by the hope of more stimulus, so the Federal Reserve and other central banks are entrapped by their own policy because they cannot retire the stimulus for fear of a market collapse from elevated valuations created by the policy itself. So, the easing policy is maintained to avoid a financial crisis caused by the unjustified valuations of financial assets created by that same policy.[8]

The Central Bank as the Pyromaniac Fireman

In the meantime, the minutes of the Federal Reserve and other central banks deny such aggressive valuations but show that the policy is prolonged due to risks in markets themselves.

The liquidity trap becomes a market trap. If markets go up excessively it cannot be stopped for fear of a financial-led recession and if markets correct it must be increased ... for fear of a financial-led recession.[9]

One of the clearest signals of this excessive risk fueled by central bank policy is margin debt, that is, the amount of debt taken by market participants and invested in stocks and bonds. It reached multiyear highs rising from 1 percent of GDP to above 2.9 percent of GDP in the United States by 2015, almost a threefold increase and double the historical median. It peaked at 2.6 percent before the financial crisis, and the average median since 1990 was 1.55 percent.

Now, this is the funny part. A massive increase of margin debt was viewed by many commentators as a risk or as a bullish signal.

The risk is evident. Too much debt is taken betting on further rise in stocks, so, if it does not happen, the ability to repay such debt collapses

---

[8] The Ultra-Easy Money Experiment, William White. Bruno Leoni Institute, Rome. October 2015.

[9] http://inflation.us/nyse-margin-debtgdp-explodes-past-dot-com-bubble-peak/

and there is a domino of payments that cannot be met, creating a financial crisis if the stock of unpayable debt is too large.[10]

However, some see it as a positive signal. Investors are more confident about the economy, corporate profits, and dividends, and therefore take more debt to invest in this trend. It sounds plausible. But it is complete garbage.

If confidence soars and profits are rising according to estimates, at least the market would become cheaper, as valuations would reflect those estimates at least one year ahead. But what happened was the opposite. The Shiller PE ratio, which measures the average price of stocks relative to their earnings, went from 15× to 27×—significantly higher than the historical average of 12× to 13×.[11]

What was happening was completely different. Markets were betting on the loss of value of money due to devaluation policies and on the relentless quest to increase inflation, generating an all-time-high bubble.

This bubble was even more evident in bonds. Central banks bought trillions of dollars of government bonds causing their yields to collapse. As the lowest risk asset yield fell to the lowest level on record, the yield of riskier assets, which is set by comparison to the lowest risk asset— the U.S. 10-year bond and the German bund—also collapsed. Suddenly, investors competed to buy bonds with much higher risk but much lower returns. Inflows into the bond market increased by almost $1 trillion between 2009 and 2014, posting an almost annual 30 percent higher inflow than historical figures showed.[12] Companies that showed almost bankruptcy-type cash flow and balance sheet were issuing bonds at rates not seen in three decades, reaching an all-time low in 2013. This race to the bottom of returns and top of risk was called "the thirst for yield."

Pension funds and mutual funds invest predominantly in bonds, the safest and more stable financial assets. Those bonds pay an annual coupon, which makes for most of the returns expected, or promised. As central

---

[10] Exactly what happened with housing and margin calls; could happen to stock markets.

[11] www.multpl.com/table

[12] Thomson Reuters 2009 to 2014.

bank-led financial repression makes safe assets yield less (in some cases even negative) every year, these pension funds have to look elsewhere for a bit of return. What do they look for? Bonds with increasingly higher risk. But those yields have also fallen. So, the portfolio of the unsuspected "long-term, low-risk investor" gradually fills up with assets whose real risk is significantly superior to the one that the investor looked for.

Of course, the reader might say that financial conditions have improved and those risky borrowers are in a better position, so the lower yield is warranted. But it simply isn't true. The ability to repay debt fell between 2009 and 2013 to levels not seen since before the financial crisis, as shown in the annual reports of the three major rating agencies.[13]

This thirst for yield meant extraordinary inflows into bonds but, at the same time, reduction in global capital expenditure and investment in the real economy. The objective of financial repression policies—trying to force investors out of cash and liquid financial assets and into productive investment—was delivering exactly the opposite effect: a reduction in annual capital expenditure growth and collapse of money velocity, with a massive increase in bond inflows.

Lower Costs Help Cut Debt, or Not?

The reader might say, and rightly so, that falling interest rates and bond yields and rising liquidity create positive effects. Debts are easier to be repaid, companies and governments finance themselves cheaper, and therefore growth is boosted.

Yes, debt is easier to be repaid, but global debt has risen to all-time peacetime highs, in absolute real terms and relative to GDP. The incentive to borrow more and use it for unproductive spending is evident in the fall of productivity, the reduction in return on capital employed, and the lower levels of growth.

The United States, for example, saw a massive debt increase of $9 trillion between 2009 and 2016 to generate $3.5 trillion of GDP. Elsewhere, the ratio of debt to additional GDP rose to 18 to one.[14]

---

[13] End of 2013 and 2014, Moody's, Standard and Poor's, Fitch.
[14] According to Deutsche Bank, 2016.

Borrowers adapt quickly to low yields, and even with collapsing rates, the cost of a shock rises as debt balloons. A very revealing case can be seen in the eurozone where countries such as Spain, Italy, or Portugal, despite issuing at the lowest rates in the historical series, would suffer an enormous debt shock only from a rise of 1 percent in the cost of debt.[15]

Reading the banks' strategists' reports of the QE period was also proof of this mentality. A constant message in recommendations to investors was to keep buying stocks expending "accommodative policies."

By 2016, an entire generation of traders and market participants had not seen anything except expansionary policies. This led to the consensus's inability to discern proper valuation opportunities and understand risk and earning cycles.

Mainstream Consensus and the Swindle of the Hockey Stick

This inability is clearest when looking at estimates of corporate profits and macroeconomic projections, which are essential to determine whether the stock market is cheap or if the economy is improving.

However, every year, especially in the past eight years, we witness an interesting pattern: massive downward revision of corporate profit expectations. These have averaged 15 percent between January and December almost every year.[16]

The mainstream consensus of analysts suffers from the same constant mistake of large international organizations, whose average accuracy in their short- and medium-term predictions is less than 26 percent, as mentioned earlier. The error of the "double trap": long-term optimism and negation of short-term trends.

If we take Bloomberg's earnings-per-share (EPS) estimates for the Euro Stoxx 50, for example, in January 2016 for that same year, these were +1.5 percent and for 2017, +12.4 percent.

---

[15] A widespread increase of 1 percent in interest rates for the eurozone would cost €10 billion in higher costs using one-year average maturities of 2016 to 2020.
[16] Bloomberg median.

If we then look at the same estimates for the same index on December 16, 2016, what do we find? Profits for 2016 are +2.3 percent and for 2017, +11.1 percent.

This trend is very similar to that of S&P: full-year profits (EPS) for 2016 fell from +2.7 percent in January to +0.1 percent in December and for FY17, from +14 percent in January to +12.3 percent in December.[17]

Note the impact on estimates in 11 months: from healthy profit to loss or no growth. But note, in turn, the gradual but inexorable erosion of expectations for the following year.

Why is this happening? The hockey stick in future estimates is the best excuse to justify blunders.

If we look at the examples in macroeconomic estimates, from the Federal Reserve[18] to the ECB[19] and the IMF, the Federal Reserve has been cutting one-year-forward estimates by up to half since 2009. What about inflation estimates? The same. In the case of the large international organizations, we are talking of mistakes of more than 50 to 70 percent in one-year estimates and over optimism in cases of recession.[20]

Ignore for a second the disaster in prediction track record, and let us focus on the shape of estimates—almost always a hockey stick. See Figure 3.2.

Suppose, as with the future estimates, that economists have failed in the current-year estimates. What is the answer? "But look, next year everything improves." And, in turn, the next hockey stick is moved to the new, lower, base. But that figure, the hockey stick of fantasy future projections, remains. Don't worry, "next year" will always be there.

There are various reasons:

Mainstream consensus tends to overestimate the positive impact of monetary policy over other risk factors. It is very evident in corporate

---

[17] Bloomberg consensus estimate of EPS.

[18] This graph shows how bad the Fed is at predicting the future, Dylan Matthews, Washington Post, June 19, 2013.

[19] Economic forecasting: some lessons from recent research. ECB Working Papers.

[20] On the Accuracy and Efficiency of IMF Forecasts: A Survey and Some Extensions, Hans Genberg and Andrew Martinez, 2014.

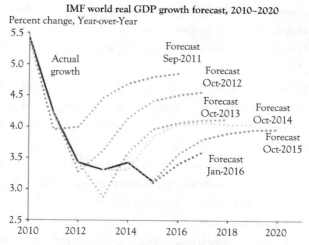

IMF world real GDP growth forecast, 2010–2020

Figure 3.2 IMF world real GDP growth over time

Source: IMF, Washington Post.

profits and even more so, in capex estimates. As noted before, capex predictions have been particularly erroneous.

Since 2012, while consensus predicted increases in real net investment, it fell, very severely in the years 2013 to 2016.

Analysis houses often introduce large impacts on GDP, consumption, unemployment, and investment or inflation expectations due to changes in monetary policy, without addressing much more relevant trends such as overcapacity, aging, technology, or the real cost of capital. The results lead invariably to downward revisions, albeit gradually—little by little, month by month—in order not to look so bad.

Denying business cycles is another mistake. Cycles become shorter and more abrupt as debt rises and money velocity falls. Using estimates where the starting point is simply moved lower and then increased annually, as if there were no cyclical factors that cancel those correlations, is a frequent mistake.

Additionally, confirmation bias is very evident in these errors in expectations. Mainstream consensus considers short-term mistakes as just anomalies—white noise that does not change the medium-term prediction—just because most peers support the starting premise and it needs to be reaffirmed.

Of course, to justify these deviations in short-term estimates, mainstream consensus will use sentences such as "there were unexpected challenges," "fundamentals have not changed," and "in the longterm it will improve."

To defend the "eternal hockey stick," there will be seemingly robust studies of regressions, endless spreadsheets, and complicated algorithms in which everything appears very scientific until we understand that most of the key "inputs" are subjective.

The general mistake in medium-term estimates comes mainly from altering the result to justify the conclusion, albeit involuntarily, due to individual prejudices, peer pressure, and ideological preferences. There are many studies that warn of the "pollution" in optimistic estimates,[21] where many of these predictions simply seek to justify an existing policy or strategy,[22] or, in the case of corporate profits, valuations that are hardly supported by fundamentals. Any analyst in the world knows that, on average, 80 percent of the valuation of a stock is explained by the years that exceed the "forecast period" (normally four, maximum five, years).

Paul Romer, chief economist of the World Bank, also criticized the perverse incentives in macroeconomics. "For more than three decades, macroeconomics has gone backwards," he states. Romer comments that most economists drift away from science, being more interested in preserving reputations than testing their theories against reality, "more committed to friends than facts," offering a wicked parody of a modern macro argument: "Assume A, assume B, ... blah blah blah ... and so we have proven that P is true."[23]

Does this mean that analysis is useless? Not at all.

Analysis has an enormous value in what we must do with the detailed study of factors that affect companies, governments, and families. But

---

[21] www.smh.com.au/federal-politics/political-opinion/when-a-guess-is-as-good-as-a-forecast-20130108-2cep8.html

[22] Growth Forecast Errors and Fiscal Multipliers, Olivier Blanchard and Daniel Leigh, IMF 2013.

[23] "The Trouble With Macroeconomics," Paul Romer. Stern School of Business New York University. September, 2016.

predictions, especially for more than three years, should be taken not with caution, but with the certainty that they are contaminated by optimism.[24]

To be guided by long-term predictions of economists that deny cycles and are clearly unable to predict the most immediate future is, at the very least, dangerous.

Making estimates is essential for economic analysis. It helps us realize where we are wrong, and act accordingly by recognizing those impacts—positive or negative—that we missed, for further analysis. Making mistakes is essential to improve. The problem is to confuse estimates with infallible magic predictions and, even worse, to cover these hockey stick estimates with a fake "scientific" layer, when they only serve as an excuse to perpetuate erroneous policies and recommendations.

The Mirage Starts to Fade

In 2009 and 2010, emerging market asset prices began to strongly inflate due to the effect of the "global carry trade" in which investors borrowed capital from deflation-prone or low-inflation countries where interest rates were too low—like the United States and Japan—and liquidity was soaring, and deployed the excess liquidity into higher-yielding investments in nondisinflation-prone economies. By late 2010, capital flows to emerging markets had risen to $825 billion—a level that exceeded the last peak during 2006 to 2007, while inflows to Asian economies rose 60 percent above their prior peak.[25]

Even Dilma Rousseff, ex-president of Brazil, decried the large pool of speculative capital that sought returns in emerging markets, calling it a "monetary tsunami"[26] due to its impact on inflation, overheating of the economy, and asset bubbles in emerging market economies. However, even she fell under the liquidity trap leading the country to a massive

---

[24] Growth Forecast Errors and Fiscal Multipliers, Olivier Blanchard and Daniel Leigh, IMF 2013.

[25] According to Bloomberg, Citigroup.

[26] https://brazilportal.wordpress.com/tag/dilma-monetary-tsunami/

overcapacity[27] and investments in large, unproductive infrastructure projects, also called white elephants.

Bubbles Happen in the Perceived Safest Assets

The problem with bubbles is exactly this. They happen in the assets and in areas that the consensus believes are less risky and the safest—housing, energy, infrastructure, government bonds—and even some of the governments and leaders who rightly identify the risk of massive unjustified inflow into an overheating market fall under its spell when time passes and their prediction of a prickling of the bubble fails to happen. They start to believe the reports of economists that speak of new paradigms, that repeat "this time it's different" … and then it happens. The bubble bursts when there is no one else left to convince that it didn't exist in the first place. See the example in oil prices versus supply in Figure 3.3.

Other examples of excess of liquidity turning into mirages and bubbles happened in Canada and Australia. Mining and oil companies always invested with a commodity deck that reflected significantly lower prices than the forward curve. Miners rarely took any debt because of the risks entailed from carrying financial burdens in a highly cyclical sector. Massive rises in commodity prices due to devaluation of the U.S. dollar and the illusion of perennial growth in China and the emerging markets added to the perception that massive liquidity and low rates would stay forever, and generated a complete change in the mind of an otherwise historically financially prudent sector.

Leveraged investments in mining and energy soared. The annual capital expenditure in Oil and Gas alone multiplied by tenfold in a little over a decade, and massive overcapacity was created from completely overoptimistic expectations of demand, prices of commodities, and cost of debt. By 2013 delinquencies in the most inefficient companies and dramatic investment program and dividend cuts had to be undertaken.

The U.S. Federal Reserve's $600 billion QE2 program, which began in the fall of 2010, caused commodities prices to surge further and resulted

---

[27] Almost 30 percent by the time she left power.

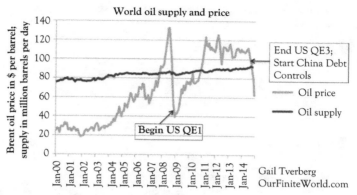

Figure 3.3 World oil supply and price vs. QE

Source: Gail Tverberg.

in a new wave of fears of economic overheating. In early 2011, Andrew Haldane, chief economist at the Bank of England, warned of emerging market asset bubbles due to capital inflows from advanced economies (see Figure 3.4), and the IMF alerted governments of overheating. Joachim Fels, chief economist at Morgan Stanley, warned that the BRIC[28] nations faced an "elevated risk of credit bubbles and rising defaults," and banks began to show the signs of a credit crisis.

Economies started to show the signs and credit downgrades ensued. Despite the slowdown in emerging market economies, their fixed income assets were still attracting massive capital inflows, but volatility started to really show an uglier face, placing many of the issuers under economic duress despite rising liquidity.

The Federal Reserve's purchase programs suppressed bond yields below their natural market-clearing level at the same time as expansive cycles proved to be shorter and more abrupt. The high growth of two to three years became, due to overcapacity and high debt into unproductive investments, the recession of the following period. Traditional and conservative buy-and-hold bond strategies become riskier. In fact, both opportunity cost risks and actual default risks escalate when bond prices are artificially high (and yields artificially lower).

---

[28] Brazil, Russia, India, China.

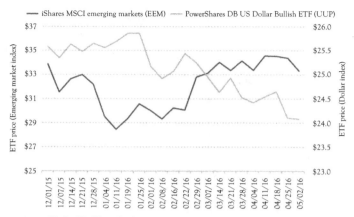

Figure 3.4 U.S. Dollar Index vs. Emerging Market Index

Source: NYSEArca.

Bondholders receive a lower return for their investments and become exposed to inflation, losing yield when they might have been better off pursuing instruments with higher upside.

This perceived risk was so strong that, during the deliberations about QE in the European Union, economists from the World Pensions Council (WPC)[29] warned that artificially low government bond interest rates could compromise the underfunding condition of pension funds. They argued that diminished returns from QE could force negative real savings rates on pensioners. In 2016, it happened: more than $11 billion in negative yield bonds worldwide.

But QE also harms liquidity in markets despite being a massive injection of—liquidity.

The aim of QE might be to increase liquidity in global markets, but it ends up having the opposite effect. Investors become more prudent, and place more of their assets in low-risk bonds and cash.

Capital increases merger and acquisition transactions; companies' floating and capital expenditure falls.[30]

---

[29] http://nebula.wsimg.com/e68d7776b95ea984eb11a1bc120e38af?AccessKeyId=9BB168F4CFBA64F592DA&disposition=0&alloworigin=1
[30] In the 2009 to 2014 period, according to Goldman Sachs and UBS.

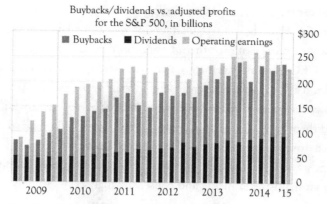

Figure 3.5 Buybacks and dividends relative to earnings

Source: Marketwatch.

Companies devoted more funds to dividends and buybacks, not doing what mainstream economists demanded them to, which was to grow,[31] because there was no real confidence in the economy. See Figure 3.5.

As Borio explains:

Attaining monetary and financial stability simultaneously has proved elusive across regimes. Edging closer toward that goal calls for incorporating systematically long-duration and disruptive financial booms and busts—financial cycles—in policy frameworks. For monetary policy, this means leaning more deliberately against booms and easing less aggressively and persistently during busts. What is ultimately at stake is the credibility of central banking—its ability to retain trust and legitimacy.[32]

---

[31] From 2009 to 2016, buybacks have tripled from $205 billion to $627 billion, and net buybacks have increased by more than $540 billion. Since February 2007, total gross buybacks have grown from $521 billion to $627 billion, and net buybacks have grown from $350 billion to $448 billion, according to Jeremy Schwartz, director of research at Wisdom Tree Investments, Inc.

[32] Claudio Borio. Monetary policy and financial stability: what role in prevention and recovery? BIS Working Papers No 440, January 2014.

And central banks are losing credibility faster than the speed of light.

Despite what the central planners of monetary laughing gas want us to see—a mirage of growth and opportunities to take risk and invest more—CEOs and management teams witnessed every day the weakness in demand and the level of overcapacity in their respective markets. Companies saw a reality different than what central banks and governments wanted them to see. Families did not see lower rates and financial repression as a driver to spend more and take credit. Because the reality in front of them was stubbornly different from the science-fiction-like improvement that mainstream media and consensus analysts desperately tried to paint.

How could anyone expect anything different, when the experience of Japan showed that the economy stalls and participants become more conservative, after 21 years of zero interest rate policies (ZIRP) and six consecutive stimulus programs? Because, as it always happens, many repeated the three favorite sentences of mainstream economics:

It could have been worse.
It was not enough.
This time it's different.

CHAPTER 4

Sudden Stop in Emerging Markets

"I can't stand up for falling down"

—Elvis Costello

Emerging markets don't emerge. I always tell this to my students. The emerging markets of today are the same countries that I studied when I was in school.

There are many reasons for this[1] statement but I will narrow it to one main, albeit highly complex, driver: using short-term foreign currency revenues to finance local investments in domestic currency. Cyclicality of commodity revenues and dependence on export growth generate periods of exuberance where politicians and policymakers ignore the risks of the cycle, entering large periods of excessive investment with questionable economic return only to face an abrupt loss of foreign currency revenues when the cycle turns. This makes boom and bust cycles more severe, and the ability to recovery from recessions is slower and more complicated. As financial crises become more frequent, as we showed before, the emerging economy's possibility of lifting itself from recession becomes harder and longer, but the impact on its main customer markets reduces its ability to recover when growth resumes.[2]

The sudden stop happens when emerging markets get used to an extraordinary and artificial increase in capital inflows and foreign

---

[1] Emerging Markets, Prospects and Challenges. Kalpana Kochhar, IMF, Oct 2013.

[2] The effect of financial crises on potential output: New empirical evidence from OECD countries. Davide Furceria, Annabelle Mourougane, Journal of Macro-economics, 2012 Volume 34, issue 3.

currencies. Using that unexpected capital, foreign exchange reserves rise dramatically and large investments are financed with long-term debt issued to a market hungry for yield and growth. Then, suddenly, when the placebo effect of QE halts, there is an abrupt flight of capital out of the emerging economies.

The risk in emerging markets is not only lower-than-expected growth but also the abrupt disruption in the flow of capital investment.

One of the consequences of monetary stimulus in recent years was an extreme inflation in risky assets. The United States exported inflation to semidollarized economies and emerging markets, and some of the favorite investments throughout the monetary expansion times were emerging market bonds. Suddenly, with the prospect of the Federal Reserve reducing its stimulus, a wave of unprecedented withdrawal of capital occurred.

Reserves of emerging markets' central banks fell by 10 percent, but financing needs increased by 7 percent and current account deficits widened.[3]

Excessive inflation and the collapse of local currencies made current account deficits soar in Latin American countries. Inflation soared to five-year highs in many developing markets.

The access to cheap credit and easy money created a liquidity excess of around $10 billion per month for emerging economies.[4] And this excess became a new norm: an inflation of nearly 150 percent in risky assets.[5]

Unfortunately, periods of excess liquidity were not used to reduce imbalances and strengthen economies, but were assumed to be a new paradigm of normality. Until the tide turned. See Figure 4.1.

The sudden stop.

The impact on economic growth and stability in emerging countries can be very relevant. The combination of high inflation, current account deficits, and loss of dollar reserves by central banks has never been a winning equation. And the three variables deteriorate very quickly.

---

[3] In 2013, the Taper Tantrum, when the U.S. Federal Reserve stopped its asset purchase program despite continuing with ultra-low rates.
[4] Additional liquidity above historical average, Goldman Sachs, 2013.
[5] EM index rise 2009 to 2013.

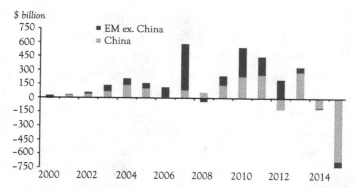

Figure 4.1 Abrupt fall in Emerging Markets Capital Flow in 2013

Source: IMF.

Indonesia lost 13 percent of its foreign reserves in three months, Turkey, Ukraine, and India showed similar figures. This is important because for many countries it is essential to hold enough dollar reserves ahead of uncertain times and financial difficulties.

Many of these countries and their companies have debt in dollars and if they hold less U.S. currency to meet their commitments, the country enters rapidly into a debt crisis.

However, when the sudden stop arrives, if central banks decide—correctly—to preserve their foreign currency reserves, devaluation hits homes and families, and inflation soars. The accumulation of imbalances generated by getting used to artificial injections of liquidity always ends in recession and high inflation.

Since 2009, Brazil, China, India, Russia, Turkey, and others have sold more than $2 trillion in bonds, mostly to American mutual fund companies.[6] As this money flowed into their countries, financing skyscrapers, massive dams, and oil exploration, economies and currencies strengthened. But then the reverse occurred, led by a slowing Chinese economy, and as that money headed for safety, local currencies collapsed.

---

[6] Moody's.

The BIS economists warned of the consequences if panicked bond investors decided to sell these positions at the same time.[7] On one side, bond funds have become so large and own so many of the same securities that a bond-selling panic can spread quickly and the price loss be more severe because the liquidity dries and the bonds become harder to sell.

About $340 billion of debt maturities accumulated between 2016 and 2018. The total payments due each year during the period is equivalent to the net bond sales by nonfinancial companies in developing nations in 2015. The danger is that once credit becomes less available, borrowing costs will rise and make it more difficult for companies to refinance their debt, according to the BIS.

The economic instability of many of these countries was not a topic of discussion at the Federal Reserve meetings throughout QE1, 2, and 3 until the world became concerned about the collapse of the Indian rupee in 2013. Many saw the risks to be small, but with soaring inflation and a widening current account deficit, risks started to arise in many other countries.

A sudden stop always has global effects. It had a relevant impact on European banks, heavily exposed to Latin America, and on multinational companies, as well as very important direct consequences in British and U.S. banks, because of their exposure to Asia and Africa. But above all, it creates challenges for developing countries with increasing refinancing needs, if they cannot access the capital markets after the boom years of the Fed "easy money."

"Significant emerging currency depreciation should cause investors to hesitate. Depreciation is a secondary form of "default."[8]

Can a sudden stop be avoided? Yes, by avoiding the previous unprecedented rise—instead of falling in the liquidity trap, using foreign currency as a tool to boost real productive investment. But which government is going to support this? When G20 countries, with a longer history of transparency and governance, fail to center capital expenditure

---

[7] www.bloomberg.com/news/articles/2016-08-18/bis-flags-emerging-market-risks-as-340-billion-of-debt-matures

[8] William H. Gross, 30th July 2015.

on productive projects with real economic return[9] and resort to white elephants and unproductive debt, how could we expect anything different from any other government?

What Happens When the Tide Turns?
The U.S. Dollar Becomes the New Gold

The wakeup call that the end of QE, first, and the rise in interest rates afterward, in 2016, have meant for global asset classes should not go unnoticed as a warning sign for the future.

Above all, these changes have large implications on the cost of debt. No one can say they had not been warned, but many governments and investors preferred to think that the Federal Reserve would continue to play the monetary laughing gas game to perpetuate imbalances that were accumulated for 16 years.

Remember that an entire generation of market participants had only seen "Buy the Dip" strategies aimed at following the "bad news is good" policy of riding the central bank wave.

This central bank-led madness brought an accumulation of more than $11 trillion in negative-yield bonds. Suddenly, a small rise in inflation expectations could create potential losses exceeding $1 trillion.[10]

The vacuum effect in the United States makes the strong dollar, supported by a small rise in interest rates, absorb liquidity from all over the world back into the United States—capital flight out of commodities and emerging markets.

In China, several companies were forced to cancel relevant bond issues due to volatility when investors demanded much higher rates. China lost 20 percent of its foreign currency reserves in 2016. This is normal; if the U.S. 10-year bond rises to a required yield of 2.5 to 2.6 percent, no one in their right mind would accept risk in countries and areas of high volatility whose differential with that U.S. bond does not compensate the risk.

---

[9] What Keynes Really Said about Deficit Spending. Elba K. Brown-Collier and Bruce E. Collier. Journal of Keynesian Economics, Vol. 17, No. 3 (Spring, 1995).
[10] Estimated losses of a rise in inflation 1 percent above bond yields, Goldman Sachs 2016.

The strength of the U.S. dollar and the slight rise in U.S. rates led the Chinese sovereign 10-year bond yield to two-year highs in 2016. In two days,[11] Chinese sovereign bonds saw the biggest price drop in eight years in the five- and ten-year bonds, leading the Chinese regulator to halt trading in futures due to some capital outflows.

Such a rise in rates and an increase in risk would not be a huge problem—after all, they are still very low rates with 3.5 percent in the 10-year bond—if China had not embarked on the brutal orgy of debt. In the 12 months, China "stabilized" its slowdown with a monstrous increase of 11.4 percent in money supply (M2) for a GDP growth of 6.2 percent with a worrisome housing bubble. Total credit granted increased in 2016 from 246.8 to 265 percent of GDP, seven months after the Chinese government announced measures to "contain" excess borrowing.

The global implications of this Chinese risk are important.

Those who argue that all this cannot continue to happen, because China accumulates more than $1.2 trillion of U.S. bonds, are wrong.

First, because China has been reducing its U.S. bond portfolio for years and had at the end of 2016 the lowest figure since 2013.

Second, because—contrary to popular belief—the main buyer of U.S. bonds is not China, but U.S. investment funds and the U.S. citizens themselves. If China were to dispose of its entire U.S. bond portfolio, the U.S. market would absorb it in just over two weeks.

I believe this could happen by 2020; the Chinese are considering blockchain technology such as Bitcoin along with Gold and all the other traditional options to avoid the impact on wealth of large devaluations. Chinese were querying the blockchain exchange owners in 2016 on how much wealth new blockchain asset classes such as bitcoin could handle in a single day.[12]

The China–U.S. issue is important because it leads to a spiral in which the world's old growth engine is in evident slowdown and faces the serious problem of losing a significant part of the more than $250

---

[11] December 2016.

[12] Driven by Chinese and Indian buyers escaping the risk of devaluation and demonetization, Bitcoin reached an all-time high of $1000 in December 2016.

billion annual trade surplus with the United States if they both enter a commercial war.

In 2016 China saw capital outflows of almost $1 trillion. These capital flights erupted in a year in which the Chinese economy added more debt than the United States, EU, and Japan combined.

The Chinese bubble was exploding in slow motion and companies and savers expatriated as much capital as possible—either via acquisitions or directly with deposits—ahead of an increased risk of massive devaluations.

A country that needed four times more debt per unit of GDP growth in 2016 than in 2008 showed a clearly unsustainable model. By 2016 China's total debt ballooned, led by semistate-owned companies and the housing bubble. China already spends almost 3 percent of GDP on interest payments.

The devaluation of currencies against the U.S. dollar showed again that the Keynesian dogma that a weak currency leads to more exports is simply incorrect.

The U.S. dollar became the new gold in the face of mounting evidence that the "beggar-thy-neighbor" policies and drowning structural problems in liquidity came to an end.

There are many who think that the U.S. economy cannot tolerate a strong dollar. I do not agree. The United States only exports 12.6 percent of GDP, and less than 30 percent of the profits of the S&P 500 come from exports.[13]

Praying to the mantra of monetary expansion and devaluation will not work if the U.S. economic policy with a new administration is aimed at strengthening the domestic market, increasing disposable income for the middle and lower classes, and ending the perverse incentives created by years of failed demand-side policies.

We should be waking up from a model based on unicorns of Keynesian multipliers to a new global paradigm where the largest and most powerful economy conducts supply-side policies.

---

[13] 2016 figures.

Ignoring that this option even exists shows us how hypnotized we are with the mirage of growth by decree and the inexistent wealth from monetary expansion. But, at the very least, the world should be prepared for the growing possibility that the placebo effect of monetary laughing gas is a thing of the past.

"Trumponomics" and the End of Currency Wars

The victory of Donald Trump in the U.S. elections was a shock to the mainstream media. More than 80 percent expected a clear victory from the Democratic candidate, Hillary Clinton. Clinton exemplified the perpetuation of demand-side policies conducted by Barack Obama and a reaffirmation of the status quo.

Donald Trump, on the opposite side, presented a combination of supply-side reforms, tax cuts, and "Buy America" policies.

The unprecedented tax cuts that were announced added to a more protective policy toward industry, and messages on renegotiation of trade deals and "Make America Great Again" were supported by the World Bank, which predicted that these reforms could "accelerate global growth,"[14] and Deutsche Bank, which stated:

"We believe that the election of Trump as the 45th President of the United States will fundamentally re-order the economic, financial, and security arrangements of the post-WW2 era, and we believe that these changes will have a significant impact on the economic performance of nations, industries, and corporates across the globe.

The defining feature of Trump's economic approach is likely to be a rebalancing of the policy mix away from the exclusive reliance on easy monetary policy toward a more balanced reliance on deregulation of economic activity, supported by an expansionary fiscal policy as a means to jump-start the U.S. economy. Incidentally, this is the same policy rebalancing that we and others have recommended for the eurozone for a number of years now. This policy will be successful in moving the U.S. economy away from low-growth secular stagnation toward significantly more buoyant performance. We would not be

---

[14] Trump Tax Cuts Could Jump-Start Global Economy, World Bank, January 2017.

taken by surprise by a doubling of the growth rate of real GDP in the United States over the next two years, nor by a further significant move up of equity valuations and a material further appreciation of the dollar.

The business background of many of the key members of President-Elect Trump's new cabinet makes it highly likely that there will be a strong and concerted emphasis on lifting the heavy regulatory burdens imposed on the U.S. business sector by the outgoing administration. We expect quick progress in reforming the corporate tax system and in rationalizing the regulation of energy, finance, environment, healthcare, labor markets, and the welfare system. These policies should help raise productivity enough to make higher growth rates sustainable in the long term after the initial stimulus wears off.

We expect the new administration to remain true to an America First approach, relying on bilateral rather than multilateral deals in trade and foreign policy. This is a United States that will be prepared to take risks, and that will re-evaluate existing arrangements under the lens 'What's in it for the United States'—rebalancing some benefits toward the United States. This approach should produce a new order that will ultimately be more stable in the sense that 'good fences make good neighbors.' However, we do note that the uncertainty about the Trump administration's policies is still large, as is the reaction of those impacted by these policies. In particular, while a strong protectionist turn by the United States is not our central scenario; such an outcome would be disruptive for global trade."[15]

There are numerous papers that support the view that the tax cuts and deregulation would help jump-start the U.S. economy.

The overwhelming evidence[16] shows that growth is more likely to accelerate by cutting corporate taxes than by spending.[17] Adding the proposal to repatriate up to $1 trillion of multinationals' overseas dollar

---

[15] David Folkerts-Landau, Chief Economist, Deutsche Bank, January 2017.

[16] Tax Foundation. Tax Cuts and Growth http://taxfoundation.org/article/what-evidence-taxes-and-growth#_ftn7

[17] Various papers support the evidence:

Taxing Top CEO Incomes www.aeaweb.org/articles?id=10.1257/aer. 20151093 "Technical Change, Wage Inequality, and Taxes," Laurence Ales, Musab Kurnaz Christopher Sleet www.aeaweb.org/articles?id=10.1257/aer.20140466

accumulation—which at the end of 2016 exceeded $2.5 trillion—would also be beneficial for the U.S. economy. A $1 trillion infrastructure investment program, financed entirely by private capital with tax deductions, would be a huge relief to the deficit with a boost on output. Although fiscal multipliers of infrastructure spending are debatable in an open economy, there is merit to the idea in the United States where infrastructure investments are clearly required.

Reducing the excess cost of healthcare, cutting red tape, and boosting disposable income through tax cuts is probably the best solution to secular stagnation.

Empirical research, from Mertens and Ravn to Alesina and Ardagna, Logan, and the IMF,[18] concludes that in more than 170 examples in history tax cuts impact growth more positively than does spending.[19]

In Trump's case those cuts mean that citizens with annual income lower than $25,000 will not pay income tax; those making less than $75,000 will pay10 percent; those making between $75,000 and $225,000, a maximum 20 percent; and those making above that, a marginal tax rate of 25 percent. This is the biggest tax cut in history.

Corporate tax would be lowered to 15 percent, with a 10 percent repatriation tax on funds accumulated offshore. Goldman Sachs estimates that the United States could repatriate more than $1 trillion with this policy.

How will these tax cuts be financed? By improving public spending efficiency, repealing and replacing the Affordable Care Act, cutting red tape, and reducing most public spending items by 1 percent a year.

The administration plans $1 trillion in infrastructure projects that would be entirely financed with private sector funds, paid via tax credits, tolls, and fees.

Some question the plan. The Peterson Institute estimated $2.85 trillion lower revenues in ten years from the tax reform, and $1 trillion of higher defense spending, leading to a 25 percent increase in debt.[20]

---

[18] http://taxfoundation.org/article/what-evidence-taxes-and-growth#_ftn7
[19] Tax cuts vs. Spending www.wsj.com/articles/SB10001424052748704271804575405311447498820
[20] Peterson Institute for International Economics, analyzing Hillary Clinton's and Donald Trump's economic plans, 2016.

On the other hand, others[21] estimate that the plan could even reduce debt.

In my own analysis, debt would fall by cutting spending by 1 percent per annum on oversized plans, which would create $750 billion savings in 10 years. Revenues from corporate tax would not fall, but stay unchanged in real terms due to the increase in economic activity and repatriation of U.S. firms' foreign investments, while wage increases would increase tax revenues. Debt to GDP would decrease with a small increase in inflation, higher growth at 2.8 percent per annum, and achievement of energy independence in 2019—eliminating barriers to exploration and production also increases real investment. Finally, the hoover effect of inflows of capital into the United States and outside of emerging markets would strengthen the economy.

After years of currency wars, one of the least talked about proposals of the Trump administration is the one that aims to penalize with economic sanctions those countries that manipulate their currency ... even the United States.

The proposal is not entirely new, and has been defended by Republicans since 2014, but the novelty is in the penalization of monetary manipulation.

On the one hand, Republicans have two proposals, one in the *House of Representatives Financial Services Committee* and another in the *Senate Banking Committee*, by which the Federal Reserve would be prevented from making decisions on interest rates and balance-sheet expansion if they deviate by more than two percentage points from a predetermined Taylor Rule.

If the Federal Reserve targets a level of inflation and employment for a level of rates and monetary policies, it would have to explain to Congress or the Senate why it changes or deflects the normalization when these targets are met.

Very few representatives of the Republican Party deny that the dramatic cut in interest rates led to a huge bubble that generated the 2008 crisis, and that prolonging the so-called expansive policies in recent years

---

[21] CFRB, Committee For Responsible Federal Budget.

has generated another bubble in bonds and an excess of euphoria in financial assets with no discernible impact on the real economy.

As we mentioned before, the indiscriminate creation of money not supported by savings is always behind the greatest crises, and there is always someone willing to justify it as both a problem and its solution.

Add to this that the economists of the Federal Reserve and its chairpersons were all unable to alert or even recognize the risk of such bubbles—from Greenspan[22] to Bernanke[23] or Yellen[24]—and you will understand why there is a growing body of politicians concerned about monetary policies that are always launched as if they had no risk and then justified with the lame argument of "it would have been worse."

Of course, the Federal Reserve rejects such limitations.[25] However, the model used to justify the stance that following a Taylor Rule would have impacted 2.5 million jobs is questionable to say the least, as it assumes a direct correlation between interest rates, money supply and investment, and job creation that simply does not work. Torsten Slok states: "If the Fed in 2008 and 2009 had followed a Taylor Rule then they would most likely have responded in the same way as they did."[26] But market participants would have been less prone to risk on the view that the Fed would do "anything." We know this because it is the way the market strategy changed after QE3.

When the central bank becomes the largest *hedge fund* in the world under the premise that there is "no inflation" despite a massive bubble in financial assets, it is difficult to change the methodology of the entity. But after it consistently erred on estimates, impact, and consequences, it is normal that the Republican Party and many Democrats put the mandate of the central bank in question.

---

[22] www.nytimes.com/2010/03/19/business/economy/19fed.html

[23] www.washingtonpost.com/wp-dyn/content/article/2005/10/26/AR2005102602255.html

[24] www.thetimes.co.uk/tto/business/markets/us/article3922666.ece

[25] medium.com/@neelkashkari/taylor-rule-would-have-kept-millions-out-of-work-9ab31fd826bf#.tccy11vcs

[26] "Audit the Fed legislation," 2nd January 2017.

Carl Icahn, one of the world's top investors and Trump's appointed regulation adviser, still holds the napkin where he took note of the Federal Reserve chairman's response to his question on whether they had gauged the negative consequences of the Fed's monetary policy. "We don't know," was the answer.

But what is interesting is the idea of penalizing countries that implement devaluation policies of beggar-thy-neighbor after the currency war seen in recent years. But the United States cannot prevent central banks of other countries from continuing to impoverish their citizens through devaluations and brutal increases in money supply ... unless they are fined for doing so. And that penalty can have dissuasive effects and, in addition, prevent the generation of larger bubbles that lead us to another financial crisis.

It is not about returning to the gold standard. In fact, what this group of representatives of the Republican Party demands—and in that they are right—is the end of uncontrolled monetary excess without any responsibility for its consequences—rejecting a system that encourages bubbles and overindebtedness under the excuse that "it could be worse."

We do not know if these measures will be implemented, but it is important and healthy that the debate over the excesses of central banks is raised at government level in the world's leading economy. Trump himself, who once said that "America can print all the money it needs," abandoned that ridiculous comment.

In any case, just as the crisis of 2008 ended the excesses of some financial operators, it is time to alert that central banks' balance sheet cannot be used indiscriminately as if they were high-risk funds to perpetuate bubbles, when the result has been more than disappointing.

Recovering a little sanity, even modestly, will not hurt anyone.

CHAPTER 5

Abenomics Fails

"You never give me your money, you only give me your funny paper"
—Lennon/McCartney

The great Nobel laureate Simon Kuznets once said: "There are four kinds of countries in the world: developed countries, undeveloped countries, Japan and Argentina." Both Japan and Argentina share only one thing in common. The two countries commit the same mistakes repeatedly, and said mistakes are always in monetary policy.

There are numerous factors that differentiate both economies, of course. I would not dare to compare them in productivity, population, technology, or competitiveness. Argentina's massive monetary imbalances erupt in monster inflation rates and devastating banking crises. Japan's slow burn comes from ballooning debt and secular stagnation.

More than 20 years of zero interest rates. See Figure 5.1.

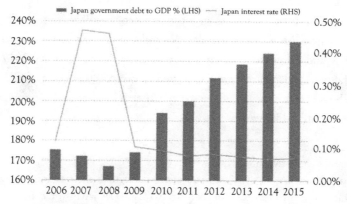

Figure 5.1 Japan: interest rates vs. government debt to GDP

Source: BoJ.

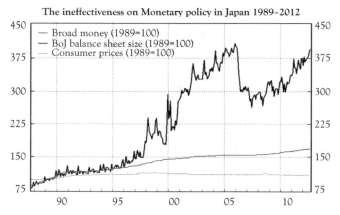

Figure 5.2 Abenomics is nothing new. Previous stimulus also failed

Source: Fulcrum, FT.

"Those who believe in Abenomics are suffering from amnesia. This is nothing new."[1] As can be seen in Figure 5.2.

Abenomics was named after prime minister Shinzō Abe. After nearly two decades of economic stagnation, the plan would launch Japan into a new era, and it was presented in December 2012 with big headlines of an ambitious and innovative policy that would change the country's fortunes. Growth, jobs, and escape from deflation.

The plan was focused on three arrows,[2] using the Japanese saying that one or two arrows can be easily broken with hands but breaking three is almost impossible.

The first arrow was an even looser monetary policy from the BoJ— nothing new. After nearly two decades and six stimulus plans, the central bank would purchase assets at a pace not seen in decades. By 2017 the central bank balance sheet was expected to exceed 90 percent of GDP.

The second arrow was nothing new either: a fiscal boost from increased spending on public works.

---

[1] Yasunari Ueno (Mizuho).

[2] Japan's three arrows of Abenomics continue to miss their targets. www.theguardian.com/business/economics-blog/2015/nov/16/japan-three-arrows-abenomics-recession-economy-targets-shinzo-abe

"From Meccano to Legoland, here they come with a brick in their hand, men with heads filled up with sand. It's build." The Housemartins

Yes, Japan spent between 1991 and 2008 a whopping $6.3 trillion in infrastructure projects to "boost growth," with an inexistent impact on economic output—the country stagnated for two decades—or on real wages. Japan's economy did not become more dynamic, but much less, after the bonanza in infrastructure.[3]

The third arrow was more ambitious: A sweeping structural reform to make the economy more productive and competitive, attacking "special interests"—corruption—and incentivizing high productivity, lower bureaucracy, and dynamism. Guess what? The third arrow was forgotten.

Shinzō Abe outlined measures such as setting up special economic zones but failed to address reforms surrounding the labor market and corporate taxes. No real reform of a bloated state, of vested interest and cronyism problems, rigid labor laws, poor margins, and inefficiencies of the system.

Some commentators mentioned that anyone expecting a broad overhaul of Japan's economy that would remove barriers to competition would likely be disappointed, and they were right. By 2016, policies seemed to be focused more in perpetuating the status quo and betting any improvements on money printing.

Jesper Koll, head of Japanese equity research at JPMorgan Chase in Tokyo stated: "You are in a country that is obsessed with creating a Japanese-style capitalism rather than market fundamentalist, Anglo-American-style capitalism. It's still Japan."[4]

So, as the reader can imagine, growth did not happen, inflation did not improve, and real wages continued to be at decade-lows while debt rose to the highest level in the OECD.

---

[3] If You Build It … Myths and realities about America's infrastructure spending. Edward L. Glaeser, 2016.

[4] CNBC comment.

It is not just public debt. Zero interest rate policies have also made private debt soar. At the end of 2016, Japan's total debt stood above 450 percent of GDP.[5]

But the reader might think, how did they get there?

Japan's All-Too-Familiar Bubble

In 1980, Japan's budget was just 45 trillion yen. Most of it was public works, government transfers, and interest payments.

Japan entered a massive boom led by construction. The stock and property markets soared, and with them the growth illusion and extraordinary tax revenues created by the bubble. Not only did Japan become richer, but its companies entered an enormous process of international expansion. It seemed like Japan would take over the world. See Figure 5.3.

This sounds familiar to any U.S., Spanish, Swedish, or now Chinese citizen … the illusion of magic revenues from housing booms. With the bubble, spending also increased, and borrowing expanded.

Then, bust … Japan's real estate bubble exploded, and the country, to reactivate the economy, did exactly what the reader has guessed—it created a massive infrastructure plan to boost growth. Expenses continued to soar, driven also by more welfare costs from aging population and accumulated interest payments from the debt incurred during the "this time it's different" boom.

Obviously, that growth did not happen, but the debt stayed. After six stimulus plans and two lost decades of deflation and almost no growth, the country presented a new plan[6] that was just the same, but bigger.

Japan's crisis was simply the pricking of a bubble in very slow motion and the perverse negative effects of decades of stimulating low-productivity sectors. This policy bloated the economy and killed its dynamism, at the public and the corporate level.

---

[5] Bloomberg.

[6] How Japan's national debt grew so large http://ritholtz.com/2013/10/how-japan%C2%92s-national-debt-grew-so-large/

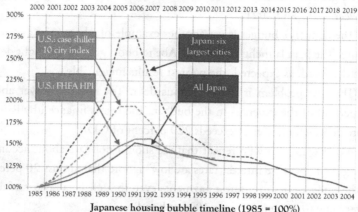

Figure 5.3 *Comparing the U.S. and Japan housing bubbles*

Source: doctorhousingbubble.com

Why Japan Is Unlikely to Change

Japanese citizens do not suffer from amnesia. The population is aware of the unlikely effect of all these measures announced as "new." And they save, a lot.

Fifty-six percent of the total wealth of Japanese citizens is accumulated in deposits and currency.[7] The government feels the urge to stick its hand in their pocket ... devaluing.

But the Japanese, like the Europeans, do not spend more. The big problem is that the velocity of money—which reflects economic activity—continues to fall despite aggressive liquidity. The lack of consumer confidence does not dissipate by manipulating monetary variables because most fears come from the fear of further increase in taxes and cost of living.

After years of stimulus, Japan published its 2017 budget on its way to another year of pauper growth and high debt.

Japan should matter to all of us. Because it is an example of what countries in the rest of the world should not do after two decades of stagnation and repeating stimulus after stimulus.

---

[7] Credit Suisse, 2013, Japan Implications.

The *Economist* places Japan again among the 20 economies with lowest growth for 2017 and estimates 0.5 percent GDP growth per year between 2017 and 2021.

The country's budget is yet another example of Abenomics as a total failure. The plan launched by Shinzō Abe to boost growth and fight deflation delivered, as expected, the poorest results imaginable.

The first problem is the enormous debt. Tax revenues cover about 60 percent of the expenses in the budget. The rest is financed by issuing more debt, which already exceeds 229 percent of GDP.[8]

Neo-Keynesians who repeat that we should not care about accumulating debt "because interest rates are low" ignore that almost 20 percent of the budget goes to interest payments even though Japan's cost of debt is very low (0.10 percent for a 10-year bond).

However, it is dangerous to ignore that the BoJ will "swallow" the vast majority of those bonds issued.

The closest thing to a Ponzi scheme?[9]

By the end of 2016 the central bank of Japan accumulated more than 35 percent of the bonds issued by the government as well as owned the largest share of ETFs[10] in the country.

The central bank of Japan was on the path to become the largest shareholder of 55 companies in the Nikkei by end of 2017 and is already one of the top five shareholders in 81 of them.[11] This is as close to a pyramid scheme as one can imagine.

Many problems affect the Japanese economy, but the largest one is that of a rapidly aging population, which is not solved by printing money. More than 40 percent of the budget goes to pensions and health care.

But above all, monetary policy and government stimulus do not guarantee pensions, which were cut again in FY 2017–18 due to the unsustainability of the system. This should be yet another warning sign to those

---

[8] Bank of Japan, Treasury Budget 2017.
[9] A Ponzi scheme is a scam by which investors are promised a strong return which is paid by the inflow of capital from new investors, not by higher profits.
[10] Exchange-Traded Funds.
[11] Filings, Bloomberg, Reuters.

who say pensions are guaranteed by raising taxes and implementing monetary policy. It does not even happen in Japan.

Of course, Japan has low unemployment, but that has been the case for decades. The combination of an aging population and cultural challenges for immigration keeps the workforce tight.

However, social security contributions fail to cover even a portion of the expenditure in public pensions. Additionally, at 36 percent, Japan has one of the lowest replacement rates in the world (the percentage of the last salary paid as public pension).

And that is the big lesson. Countries try to solve with monetary measures the impact of much more relevant trends, such as demographics. Increasing taxes and disguising the problem and introducing massive useless stimulus plans only postpones the inevitable crisis.

Some might say "who cares" because there is no inflation. However, real wages in Japan are at a two-decade low and disposable income continues to erode.

The only real beneficiary of Japan's monetary mirage—which is a slow robbery of the saver under the false pretense of the "social contract"[12]—is the government, which keeps increasing debt without addressing structural reforms, the challenges of productivity, and "special interests."

The Justification

There is a small, but relevant, group of economists that justify this policy on various grounds.

The first is the social contract. Debt does not matter because if it preserves low unemployment and high welfares spending it is a success, and the cost is very low because it is almost fully monetized.

The second is the magic of making debt disappear through monetization. On one side, debt in private hands is falling rapidly. On the other, the government never has to repay this debt.

There would be a merit to this if the reality of stagnation did not come back to bite.

---

[12] The social contract is supposed to be the guarantee that future generations will continue to support the costs of welfare and repay the debt.

The argument is that the effective public borrowing burden is plunging by as much as the equivalent of 15 percentage points of GDP a year. The government debt is shifting from private hands to the central bank. As such, the "debt excluding the QE stock" would be falling. Magic.

It just does not work.

First, even with this argument and ultralow rates, the government spends an extraordinary amount of funds from the budget—almost a quarter—and more than 40 percent of tax revenue on interest payments. And this with a policy of almost zero interest rates for two decades.

Even if we assume low inflation and no other distortions, this extraordinary expense means more taxes in the future and weaker growth.

But it does not work either as a "hide risk under the carpet" argument. It makes the BoJ's role as a massive hedge fund, self-perpetuating. If the BoJ stopped or even reduced the pace of asset purchases, the marginal buyer is more than questionable. See Figure 5.4.

Who would buy Japanese 10-year bonds at close-to-zero coupon if the BoJ would not be a guarantee of buyer of last resort? But, more importantly, which investor would buy Japanese equities with weak earnings, poor return on invested capital, and low growth if the central bank stopped buying? Of course, there would be a marginal buyer, but at significantly lower valuations than today. It is not a counterfactual

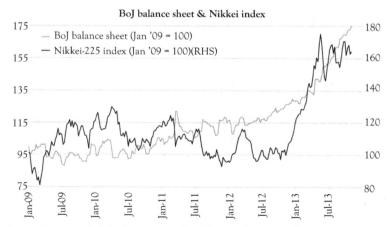

Figure 5.4 Nikkei Index vs. Bank of Japan balance sheet

Source: BoJ, Bloomberg.

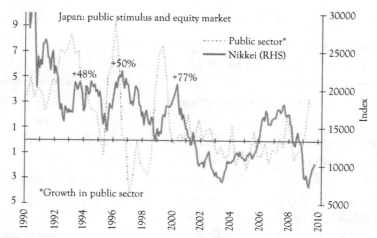

Figure 5.5 *Correlation of the Nikkei index with public-sector spending in the stimulus before Abenomics*

Source: Trading economics.

assumption. It is a proven historical fact that the stock market plunges when stimulus fades. See Figure 5.5.

There is no "hiding under the carpet" such an imbalance. The same argument was used about hedge funds and the housing bubble, when commentators believed that syndication and spreading the risk made it less evident. This massive problem will explode. It is just being artificially postponed.

The Demographic Time Bomb

Japan's nominal GDP growth has been virtually zero in the last 25 years, while public debt has tripled to 230 percent of GDP.

Although Japan pays very little, circa 0.1 percent, for its 10-year bonds, interest payments take almost 22 percent of the budget.

We mentioned the demographic time bomb. Japan has been losing inhabitants for years, and in 2016 had the lowest population since 2000. Not only does it lose inhabitants, but it ages very fast. The segment between 15 and 65 years has fallen by four million people since 2008, while inhabitants older than 65 have increased by the same number. That is why the country spends almost 30 percent of the budget in social security and pensions.

But there is another relevant factor in the corporate structure.

The Corporate Status Quo

Japan's corporate landscape is comprised of a few large industrial conglomerates, many created in the prewar period with strong ties to the emperor and the government, and 90 percent SMEs, which employ around 70 percent of the private labor force.

The corporate structure is still predominantly divided between the Zaibatsu—large industrial conglomerates—and the Keiretsu—subcontractors—which jointly, and according to many commentators, create a powerful force of intertwined interests with the government, aimed at providing stability and a joint country strategy and helping one another in different matters through time. The "special interests"—kept and supported because, at the same time, all of them have a commitment to labor stability and social welfare.

According to professor Michihiro[13] these Zaibatsu remain interlinked horizontally. Before the Second World War, many had strong ties to the military industry, and were dismantled by the U.S. Army, reviving as oligopolies after the war. There were four of these: Mitsui, Mitsubishi, Sumitomo, and Yasuda.

As a side note, the common perception that in some ways the war and the military industry were main contributors to innovation is simply exaggeration. Yes, for example, the Internet and Silicon Valley were a direct result of World War II and the Cold War, but then so were the atom bomb and nuclear weapons. Motor companies thrived during wars and after. Examples of this questionable link exist in Thyssen and Georg von Siemens in Germany; in Henry Ford, Alfred Sloan, and the two Thomas J. Watsons in the United States; and, in Sakichi Toyoda, Masatoshi Ito, and Toshifumi Suzuki in Japan.[14]

This old-school approach to sociopolitical capitalism worked for a time. It has not done so for more than two decades now. While stability exists, it can easily be confused with obsolescence, and social welfare

---

[13] Sindo Michihiro: Japanese management in capitalist Japan (1994).

[14] Creating Modern Capitalism, How Entrepreneurs, Companies, and Countries Triumphed in Three Industrial Revolutions. Thomas K. McCraw. Harvard University Press, 1998.

commitments remain at odds with impoverishment in real wages and a very hard working environment.

This formula of large conglomerates with subcontracting vertical ties to other groups gave the Japanese capitalism strength, a single purpose, and extreme loyalty from workers. But such a model cannot last when the priorities shift from growth and productivity to fighting to keep the system at any cost.

In the book *The Fable of the Keiretsu*[15] we can see that the corporate model is not too different from the French *economie dirigée* or the Spanish and Italian conglomerates with large banking shareholders.

This model of creating large conglomerates from semistate-owned companies and with blocking minority shareholders, which works as the "poison pill,"[16] is also typical in Europe. Since 2001 these models have proven to provide neither growth nor stability.

These structural problems are not covered by printing money. In fact, it makes them worse. When real wages sink, the ability of young generations to spend, have children, and improve economic activity also collapses.

Japan's solution is easy and at the same time impossible: Completely halt the corporate-financial-government chain of perverse incentives and the unproductive stimulus, concentrate on supply-side policies, lower taxes, cut red tape, and facilitate SME growth as SMEs represent 90 percent of the companies and 70 percent of jobs; such measures attract foreign investment and external workforce. But cultural and historical disincentives weigh too much.

We should see Japan as a warning sign, because the EU is copying the same mistakes but without Japan's labor discipline and technology.

---

[15] The Fable of the Keiretsu: Urban Legends of the Japanese Economy, Yoshiro Miwa, J. Mark Ramseyer.

[16] Poison pill: Corporate structure in which the Company is impossible to be taken over not because of its strength, but because of a blocking minority of shareholders with same interests.

CHAPTER 6

Draghi Comes to the Rescue

"Caroline says, as she gets up from the floor, you can hit me all you want, but I don't love you anymore"

—Lou Reed

As we mentioned before, the eurozone has some interesting similarities with Japan, and many differences, of course. The similarities are an aging population and a corporate structure that resembles a lot the Zaibatsu–Government ties.

That's probably where the similarities end. But those two factors matter, as we will see later.

There is a third factor that reduces any expected positive impact of monetary policies, and that we mentioned before: overcapacity. See Figure 6.1.

Low capacity utilization is often regarded by mainstream economists as a problem of demand that needs to be "stimulated." However, paying closer attention to the data shows the opposite.

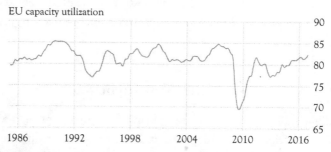

Figure 6.1 Capacity utilization in the EU has not improved despite years of industrial plans and credit boom

Source: Eurostat, Trading Economics.

Stimulating demand is precisely what the EU has been doing since the project and creation of the common currency.

Credit soared, with loans to the private sector rising 225 percent between 1999 and 2008. Public investment to GDP averaged 3 percent every year during the period. In the same period, money supply more than doubled while government-spend-to-GDP never fell below 44 percent. Household debt rose from 45 percent of GDP to 63 percent. A problem of demand stimulus? Really?

A credit boom fueled by illusions of a high-growth union and low interest rates that the central bank almost halved while doubling its balance sheet.

The eurozone crisis was exactly like all the ones we had seen before, a massive credit bubble that exploded.

And when the bubble burst, everyone blamed anything except ... themselves.

Speculators were blamed for stocks falling and bond yields rising. No one seemed to worry about them when markets soared.

Governments and politicians blamed private debt.

Households blamed banks.

No one seemed to ask, "How will we repay this ever-rising debt if growth stops?"

And, finally, some countries blamed the currency. If they had not been in the euro they would have devalued and everything would be fine. Except none of those countries asked themselves if the level of spending, investment, and development achieved within the common currency would have been feasible with their domestic currencies. It seemed everyone liked being attached to Germany for the boom, but not for the sobering bust.

Trichet Was Right

Incredibly enough, in Europe many blamed the president of the ECB, Jean-Claude Trichet, for raising rates in 2011 when the credit excess was becoming not only evident, but dangerous.

The media and mainstream economists considered raising rates at that time a mistake, as it happened in the middle of a debt crisis. But

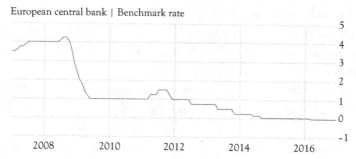

European central bank | Benchmark rate

Figure 6.2 European central bank benchmark rate

Source: ECB.

raising rates to ... 1.5 percent? That *was* the "big mistake"? Seriously? See Figure 6.2.

Interest rates were at 4.75 percent in 2000; they were lowered to 1 percent, raising rates twice a quarter of a point to a mere 1.5 percent after a massive credit boom and excess capacity, and after governments had increased debt in some cases by more than 100 percent.

Yes, there was a crisis. The decision to increase rates came at the same time as the eurozone was preparing bailouts for Greece and Portugal. But rates had been cut to historical lows and if anyone believed that 50 basis points would make a difference, they were simply fooling themselves.

Cheap Money Is Not the Answer

The eurozone crisis was not going to be solved with much lower rates.

Let us remember that, when the U.S. subprime crisis erupted, the UK financial system entered turmoil and the ripple effects were seen all over a world that had grown used to massive credit growth and low rates, the EU prided itself on being somewhat isolated from the whole financial tsunami.

Spanish banks, for example, were praised for having better regulation and thus escaping the financial crisis.[1]

---

[1] Spanish Boom and Bust and Macroprudential policy. Ángel Estrada and Jesús Saurina, Banco de España (BdE), 2016.

To combat what the media called "a financial crisis that originated in the United States" and had nothing to do with the eurozone, interest rates were dropped massively and the balance sheet of the ECB increased by €1 trillion, supporting sovereign bonds.

Additionally, the EU embarked on a disastrous "stimulus plan" that further increased the risks without any discernible growth. On November 26, 2008, the "plan for employment and growth" was launched, an ambitious project to "relaunch the economy" and create "millions" of jobs from public investment.[2]

To combat the crisis, a stimulus of 1.5 percent of GDP, more than €200 billion, was implemented—unproductive investment in white elephants and "strategic" sectors as had been done during a decade of industrial plans. Stimulate demand. White elephants had to be replaced with … white elephants.

- Spain spent €90 billion on infrastructure and civil works projects with a negative impact on both GDP and employment, as well as a debt shock.
- The EU set out to spend €200 billion and on the way destroyed 4.5 million jobs, increasing the deficit to 4.1 percent of GDP.
- The only countries that reduced taxes as stimulus were the Netherlands and the UK. Not surprisingly, they were the ones that got out of recession earlier.

This stimulus plan is still felt throughout Europe. Empty motorways next to each other, useless airports, deserted "technology centers," enormous empty buildings, industrial areas without any business activity, and so forth.

Industrial overcapacity soared, as did debt, but not growth or revenues.

The eurozone sovereign crisis continued to explode because imbalances that had been widening for more than a decade were starting to become evident. The eurozone was built under the premise that public

---

[2] http://ec.europa.eu/economy_finance/articles/eu_economic_situation/article13502_en.htm

Chart 3: Total banking assets as % of GDP

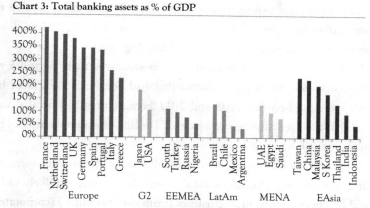

Figure 6.3 Total banking assets as a percentage of GDP

Source: Merrill Lynch; central banks.

debt had no risk,[3] and woke up to the harsh reality that risk is not decided by a committee of politicians. Credit Default Swaps (CDS), the instruments that cover the risk of default on bonds, exploded in price all over the eurozone as the massive bubble of corporate, banking, and sovereign debt pricked throughout the countries. On top of the evident risks, the concerns of a euro breakup—fueled by some reckless politicians and many unrealistic economists—made alarms ring all over Europe.

European banks, which were supposed to be extremely regulated and adequately capitalized, showed that it was all a mirage and the amount of real nonperforming loans became more evident.[4] Suddenly, the propaganda that it was all a U.S. problem of nonregulation presented a harsher reality.

Total banking assets in the eurozone exceeded 320 percent of GDP. See Figure 6.3. At the peak of the crisis, in the United States, these were 80 percent.

Furthermore, banks that were loaded with sovereign debt from their own country and from others, found it increasingly difficult to lend and borrow as well. The insurance to cover possible defaults (CDS) continued to rise as financial entities tried on one hand to reduce exposure to government bonds and at the same time maintain core capital.

---

[3] Explicitly men.
[4] More than 200 billion euro in 2010–12, ECB figures.

As I mentioned before, risk appears suddenly, and abruptly, due to accumulation of exposure to an asset that seems very safe. Public debt, government infrastructure projects, and housing.

Banks were unable to contain the bloodbath in their portfolio of assets; stocks fell, while governments that had been increasing debt by deficit spending between 2008 and 2011 because they had fiscal space, found that their refinancing costs soared. The link of external risks can be seen in Figure 6.4.

As the banks lost capital with the collapse of the value of some of their assets, sovereign bonds, loans that were increasingly unlikely to be repaid by governments, municipalities (from the "stimulus"), corporates,

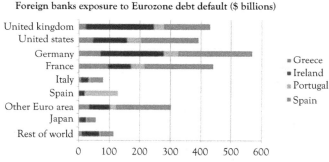

Figure 6.4 Exposure to Eurozone sovereign debt, 2011

Source: BIS.

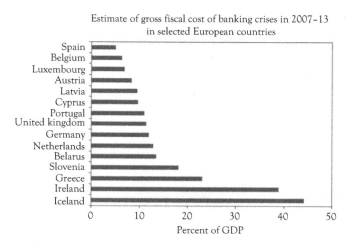

Figure 6.5 Europe bailout costs, 2016

Source: Elva Bova, IMF.

and families, the risk of a bank run led to widespread bailouts to avoid a collapse of the deposits of clients and a financial collapse. See Figure 6.5.

Many believed that devaluing would be the solution to years of excess, forgetting the devastating results of competitive devaluations of the decades before the common currency, which we mentioned in previous chapters.

The ECB's Unjust Reputation

Media and politicians always blamed the ECB for not doing as much as the Federal Reserve because, historically, the EU had denied its imbalances and risks by covering them with more credit and the layer of monetary policy.

However, by 2013, at $3.5 trillion, the Fed's balance sheet was very similar to that of the ECB. The ECB had increased its balance sheet by $1.5 trillion in four years, including €218 billion in sovereign bond purchases.

In 2013 BNP Paribas published a very revealing report titled *Bigger than QE* showing how the ECB's policy had flooded the system with credit. The main beneficiaries of this policy were Italy and Spain, two of the countries that complained the most about ECB "inaction."

Money supply (M3) reached a maximum of €9.7 trillion in January 2013 compared with an average of €0.33 trillion from 1980 to 2012, per data from the ECB. Nearly all of this increase in money supply went to one item: "Credit to General Government."

Surprisingly, the ECB had been as aggressive as the Federal Reserve, just silent. And that was the problem for market participants: the lack of big announcements that would drive markets soaring again.

All that liquidity had been absorbed between hypertrophied governments and banks buying sovereign debt, but little went to businesses and families, as deleverage continued.

The transmission mechanism problem that prevented liquidity from reaching to the real economy came partially from an unintended perverse incentive in regulation, as sovereign debt was accounted as no-risk, while lending to corporates and families was penalized with higher capital requirements. Neither Germany nor the Bundesbank, which had two-thirds of its balance sheet exposed to the ECB, were to blame. It is hard to believe they had any interest in seeing things get worse.

But the ECB, Germany, or the Bundesbank could not just sit down and maintain unsustainable economies without reforms.

There are perverse incentives in providing endless liquidity to countries that play the game of reaching the limit without reforms, wait to be systemic, get a bailout, and continue without changing bloated state structures, using the checkbook of others.

The EU was built on the premise of solidarity. But solidarity is one thing; donation is another. Especially when debt in northern countries was not low, with debt-to-GDP ratio of 80 percent and their own banking problems, doubling the bet on the periphery spending would have been suicidal after seeing the disastrous results of the previous "stimulus" of 2007 to 2011.

Greece. The Example of What Not to Do

The Greek drama unfolded and put pressure on European markets all throughout the years 2008 to 2016.

The real drama is that none of the measures announced by different parties solved Greece's real issues.

No, it was not the euro or austerity plans that crippled the Greek economy, neither was it the cost or maturity of debt. Greece pays less than 2.6 percent of GDP in interest and has 16.5 years of average maturity in its bonds.[5] In fact, Greece already enjoys much better debt terms than any sovereign restructuring seen in recent history.

Greece's problem is not one of solidarity either. Greece received the equivalent of 214 percent of its GDP in aid from the eurozone, ten times more, relative to GDP, than Germany did after the Second World War.[6]

Greece's challenge is and has always been one of competitiveness and bureaucratic impediments to creating businesses and jobs.

---

[5] 2016.

[6] Germany, Greece, and the Marshall Plan, a riposte, Jun 21st 2012, Hans Werner Sinn | IFO Institute.

Greece ranks 81 in the Global Competitiveness Index 2015, much higher than Spain (35), Portugal (36), or Italy (49). In fact, it has the levels of competitiveness of Algeria or Iran, not of an OECD country. On top of that, Greece has one of the worst fiscal systems and limits job creation with a combination of high bureaucracy and aggressive taxation on SMEs. Greece ranks among the poorest countries of the OECD in ease of doing business[7] at 61, well below Spain, Italy, or Portugal.

Greece's average annual deficit in the decade before it entered the euro was already higher than 6 percent, and in the period, it still grew significantly below the average of the EU countries and peripheral Europe.

Between 1976 and 2012 the number of civil servants multiplied by three while the private-sector workforce grew just 25 percent. This, added to more than 70 loss-making public companies and a government-spend-to-GDP figure that has averaged 49 percent since 2004, is the real Greek drama, and one that will not be solved easily.

The Greek crisis will not finish by increasing taxes to businesses, or by making small adjustments to a pension system that remains outdated and miles away from those of other European countries. A 12 percent "one-off" tax on companies generating profits of more than €500,000 crippled job creation and incentivized tax fraud.

The inefficacy of subsequent Greek governments and Troika proposals is that they never tackle competitiveness and help job creation, they simply dig the hole deeper by raising taxes and allowing wasteful spend to go on.

From a market perspective the risk was undeniably contained with the ECB's support, but not inexistent. Less than 15 percent of Greek debt in 2016 was in the hands of private investors. Most of the country's debt was held by the IMF, the ECB, and EU countries. The most impacted by a Greek default would be Germany, which held bonds of the Hellenic Republic equivalent to 2.4 percent of its GDP, and Spain, at 2.8 percent of GDP.

---

[7] Doing Business, World Bank, 2015.

The main risk for the eurozone comes from a prolonged period of no solutions. Not Greece leaving the eurozone, but a "Greek Drag," dragging on for months with half-baked attempts to sort the liquidity crisis.

Spain. An Example of Reforms That Work

On the other hand, the Spanish recovery from the worst crisis in decades was impressive. In five years, from 2011 to 2016, Spain could recover more than half of the jobs lost during a crisis that was initially denied, and deepened afterward, by misguided policies.

Since then, Spain slashed its fiscal deficit by half and cut a dangerously high trade deficit to almost a balance. Exports rose to 33 percent of GDP despite its largest trade partners being stagnant or in recession in the period.

Support from the ECB, low interest rates, and cheap oil prices helped the economy, but those factors have also helped European neighbors like Italy, Portugal, or Greece, with similar sensitivities to energy and interest rates—and none showed the growth and recovery seen in Spain.

The reason for the difference in performance of Spain relative to other neighboring countries was a very ambitious set of structural reforms that were praised as an example for others by Mario Draghi: a financial reform that helped change the perception of risk of the Spanish financial system, a labor market reform that turned around a seemingly unstoppable trend of unemployment and recovered jobs and salaries, a moderation in government spending without reducing social expenditures, and a fiscal reform in 2015 that reduced corporate and income taxes.

The remaining imbalances of the Spanish economy—an elevated public debt, deficit that is still large, and unemployment—will not be solved with monetary policies, but by learning from the economies that emerged from the crisis stronger, such as the UK, Ireland, and Germany, and with higher job creation. The measures that would strengthen the economy further should include supply-side reforms, attracting foreign investment, putting more money in companies and in citizens' pockets, and improving public sector efficiency while retaining a strong but sustainable welfare system.

ECB Launches QE

On November 1, 2011, Mario Draghi began his term as president of the ECB.

His position as president has always been supportive of expansionary policies but warning of risks and reminding of the need to conduct structural reforms and cut taxes.

Since 2015, the ECB has carried out a massive monetary stimulus—asset purchases of more than €60 million a month and zero interest rates—with more than disappointing results. However, like Trichet before him, Draghi cannot be criticized for his work, which has been exemplary in avoiding risks, calming the periods of panic, and reminding politicians and media with fastidious insistence that "monetary policy does not work without reforms."

The ECB stimulus plan has led to the balance sheet of the central bank to surpass that of the Federal Reserve, as shown in Figure 6.6.

Before that, the ECB had carried out the most logical policy of all OECD central banks. It had taken advantage of a period of excess liquidity to reduce its balance sheet, which had inflated disproportionately between 2005 and 2011, while maintaining the total credit to the system. The surplus liquidity showed that the problem was not of stimuli but of excess of indebtedness and overcapacity.

Mario Draghi has been prudent enough to warn of the mistakes of governments that rely only on monetary policy while at the same time putting the necessary tools available so that no one accused him of not supporting the economy.

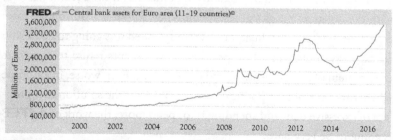

Figure 6.6 ECB balance sheet, all assets (2016, FRED)

The ECB started buying up €60 billion of assets per month, in many cases reaching more than 100 percent of demand for some bond issuances; it then increased the program to €80 billion per month. Excess liquidity increased from €75 billion to more than €1 trillion.

No one can accuse Draghi of not applying the extraordinary policies that mainstream economists and media demanded. He showed month after month that growth problems are not solved with more liquidly, that inflation is not created by a committee's decision, and that the central bank does not print growth.

By the end of 2016, the EU showed that, since 2011, it needed two additional units of debt to create a unit of GDP.

Draghi's challenge was to show that the monetary policy transfer mechanism worked and that the central bank was not to blame for poor credit and GDP growth. The improvement in the spreads between the cost of debt for states and companies, especially SMEs, was unquestionable, yet credit flow was still subdued. Because there was no real demand.

In addition, the crowding-out effect that made governments absorb almost all available credit between 2011 and 2013 moderated, with credit growth to private nonfinancial sectors growing close to 3 percent in Draghi's mandate.

The Perverse Incentives

But Draghi's biggest challenge will be how to get out of an expansive policy.

It is easy to start and buy billions of bonds, but if the Federal Reserve, with the dollar as the global reserve currency, found it hard to raise rates from 0 to 0.25 percent, imagine how complicated it is going to be to stop an expansive policy in a Europe where governments refuse to recognize the problem of excess spending and poor growth. Even worse, in a Europe where three out of four political parties think that the solution to a problem of excessive debt and spending is to spend more, the work of the ECB is going to be very hard.

That is why Mario Draghi always repeated the same words: "the ECB's policy will remain accommodative as long as necessary, but it cannot replace government inaction or undercapitalized banks." And he was right. Monetary policy is not a substitute for inefficiencies.

The construction of the EU cannot come from the same mistakes of the past, because the domino effect of systemic risk makes Europe weaker and more indebted.

Despite the messages from the ECB president, perverse incentives remain. Banks' refinancing endlessly their more troubled loans due to low rates and high liquidity means that the figure of nonperforming loans does not fall, leading to new banking crises seen in Portugal and Italy, after Cyprus and Greece.

Governments getting used to extremely favorable, but artificial, conditions means that politicians demand more expenditure, and deficits, although falling, remain elevated, with refinancing needs exceeding €1 trillion per annum for 2017 and 2018.[8]

Countries that have not seen clear improvements in their financial situation, and have increased their debt, are otherwise issuing debt at the lowest rates in the historical series. This policy of ignoring risk and increasing imbalances when rates are low and credit is available leads to chronic sovereign debt crises.[9]

Countries must be aware of the risk of a shock as the central bank is purchasing between 50 and 70 percent of all the debt that they are issuing, and it is more than unclear if any private marginal buyer would step in to purchase debt at such low rates if the central bank finishes its easing program.

Full Monetization of the Debt Is Suicidal

Debt monetization has a domino effect. It spurs foreign investors to sell domestic currencies, as money supply exceeds real GDP by many multiples, to cover ever-growing public-sector expenses, leading to a disproportionate burst in inflation.

Out-of-control inflation harms the ability of businesses to sell their goods and services because margins fall and they cannot increase prices

---

[8] Total refinancing needs, not net financial requirements. Source Bloomberg.
[9] Chronic Sovereign Debt Crises in the Eurozone, 2010–2012, TJ. Kehoe, C. Arellano, J. C. Conesa, Federal Reserve of Minneapolis, May 29, 2012.

at the pace of inflation, because citizens' real salaries do not grow in line with said inflation and purchasing power collapses.

Inputs in the economy become more expensive and, in many cases, sellers will not accept the local currency because of its volatility and constant devaluation, leading to a loss of foreign reserves from the central bank, which, in turn, leads to a larger devaluation as the new currency issued is unable to cover the needs of the country in real terms.

There is a very fine line between the central bank's credibility and the use of a currency as a credible means of transaction. The euro is used in less than 20 percent of global transactions, and its position as a reserve currency, its value to the world, is not decided by a committee.

Those who defend full monetization know that it is devastating for families and the private sector, but—like the socialist monetarists of Argentina and Venezuela—are willing to accept those damages to the economy because, in exchange, the power of the public sector soars, albeit in a much smaller and less productive economy.

That is why the central banks that conduct expansionary policies and at the same time remain solid economies are always keeping in mind the importance of a secondary market and put inflow of capital into their economies as a key driver.

A central bank that issues a currency that no one accepts as means of payment is as effective as a business that creates a product that is not demanded. A recipe for bankruptcy.

Challenges Ahead

The most dangerous policy is to increase deficits in a low-rate environment. Neither the expected growth is generated nor is one prepared for future rate increases. And the problem is that the mismatch in liabilities and revenues is covered with either higher taxes or a financial crisis, or with an inflation that destroys the purchasing power of citizens, and alongside, the potential for growth.

When we look at debt risk we must analyze two variables. Stock and flow. If confidence is maintained in our solvency and structural improvements are introduced that make the economy more solid and competitive, the stock—the total amount of debt issued—is not at risk; if prices of goods and services rise due to better consumption and productivity, neither is at risk. If markets question the ability to repay the debt maturities, and prices rise only due to monetary intervention, creating stagflation, the risk in a sell-off in the stock of debt is important.

But the flow of new issuances is very important. EU countries have done a great job improving the average life of their debt while reducing their net financing needs, but it is not enough given the large imbalances. If countries once again accelerate annual financing needs by increasing deficits, they put at risk not only their capacity for financing but also the cost—even if they have the ECB's support. A clear case is Portugal, which has the same support from the ECB as other countries, and its risk premium is over three times higher than that of Spain.[10]

Countries need to pay attention to the risk of accumulation of debt. Entering a deficit spiral would generate many more cuts when the rates rise. If we meet in 2017, we will be far from that risk. If we go back to the policies of 2010, we launch into a crisis.

Many risks persist from an aggressive monetary policy, but the ECB must be praised at least for constantly monitoring the risk of bubbles and repeating the need for structural reforms to boost growth.

The ECB shows how a central bank can learn from its mistakes and help in unforeseen risk circumstances. But it also needs to advance rapidly in improving credibility through more conservative and realistic forecasting while paying less attention to financial markets.

---

[10] Risk Premium is the differential between the German bond yield, considered the lowest risk, and the bond yield of the country.

CHAPTER 7

Zombification of the Economy ... Let's Repeat

"Maybe it's all part of a plan, I'll just keep on making the same mistakes hoping that you'll understand"

—Ed Sheeran

The vast majority of monetary policy mistakes come from denying structural issues or trying to solve those without addressing them.

Imagine a plumber that tries to fix a leak by painting the walls and trimming the garden. The house looks nice; the leak is still there.

Another of the monetary policy mistakes is to assume that recessions are caused by lack of liquidity and credit, and not by the excess of the past.

Imagine an alcoholic that goes to the doctor and says how terribly he feels sobering, and the doctor prescribes a dose of vodka and a few beers.

But it is not a joke.

The mantras repeated by consensus simply do not work.

"Devaluation boosts competitiveness and exports."

With more than 20 central banks conducting beggar-thy-neighbor policies—trying to devalue their currencies to export more—global trade has stalled.

In the eurozone, exports stalled after rising when the euro was "too expensive," as we show on Figure 7.1, just as devaluation policies were implemented.

It is clearly a global issue, driven by the increase in protectionist measures since 2008, led by antitrade policies of the United States, Russia, and China, among others, according to 2016 data from GIS. Stagnation in global trade, however, has stronger ramifications.

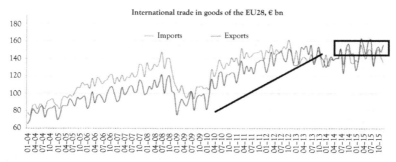

Figure 7.1 Euro area international trade before and since QE

Source: Eurostat.

Part of the increase in protectionist measures comes precisely from the mutual accusations of currency manipulation.

Even between countries that did not increase barriers to trade, exports did not improve due to weakening of the currency.

No country's economy has ever collapsed due to a strong currency. Many have due to a weakening one.

Currency Wars. No One Wins

"Devaluation rarely helps the economy, but it can help investors"
—Matt Lynn

A currency war happens when the explicit policy of a country's central bank is to devalue at any cost and its competitor nations follow the same strategy.

Devaluation. Looks like a great idea. Competitiveness "improves," debt "disappears" as the currency in which it is denominated loses value, and everything starts again. Well, no.

Because the fundamentals of the economy do not change, and credibility of governments and the financial system collapses, destroying the economy. This pyramid scheme does not work without confidence.

Since 2010, most Asian and OECD central banks have engaged in some form of aggressive currency manipulation scheme: increasing money supply, selling currency, lowering interest rates, hoarding gold or U.S. dollars, and so forth.

In this race to zero, once you pop, there is no stop. It is estimated that since 2013 central banks have expanded their balance by 15 percent per annum.

Consequences of a currency war:

One effect of this currency war is the investors' pursuit of yield at any cost to compensate for the fear of the loss of value of money. That is, less interest accepted for higher risk.

Unemployment does not improve, and work conditions worsen. It still amazes me to read that some people think that monetizing debt creates jobs.

Unemployment is reduced when economic activity recovers, when we see real productive private investment. When we create a monetary bubble, the effect is counterproductive, because money is invested in short-term financial assets and real investment falls.

Central banks will penalize investors for being conservative. But these, in turn, do not put money to work for 15 years, and less so in real assets, until they see a secure environment and growth opportunities. Money goes to the place that central banks are going to support until their final defeat: financial risky assets.

In the meantime, labor conditions weaken and real wages stall, sending the troubling signal of a level of unemployment that might appear low but where citizens struggle increasingly to make ends meet. The destruction of the middle class.[1]

As there is less job security because businesses are unable to find a stable long-term environment, disposable income falls, because real salaries do not increase but taxes do.

"Currency devaluation is merely a transfer of wealth from all of a nation's citizens to politically favored industries, usually export industries. It is no different from giving a subsidy to any domestic producer. The subsidy is paid by all the citizens of the subsidizing country, not by the foreigners who buy the subsidized good. They get a bargain.

---

[1] 30 Facts That Prove The American Middle-Class Is Being Destroyed, Tyler Durden, Aug 21, 2014.

> *Furthermore, devaluation does not make a nation more competi-*
> *tive. It does nothing to spur increased domestic saving or external*
> *capital investment, which lead to the increased application of capital*
> *per capita, the only sources of increased worker productivity and the*
> *only sources of increased real wages. Devaluation does not reveal the*
> *onerous, wealth-destroying effect of economic regulation, not does it*
> *reveal the true costs of the welfare state, which relies on high taxes to*
> *fund present consumption at the expense of future prosperity. What*
> *the state spends cannot be saved and invested, no matter how cheap*
> *the currency."*

—Patrick Barron

The main risk of widespread devaluation is global stagnation caused by the fall of productive investment and real disposable income.

How do investors profit from currency wars? Through energy commodities, physical gold, Bitcoin, and inflation-linked asset-backed securities. It is called the inflation hedge. Anything whose market value increases due to the weakening of the currency.

Cheap Money Calls for Cheap Debt

We have already seen that massive stimulus and low rates have not reduced debt. Total gross debt has continued to rise at a dangerous pace.

Because, when talking about debt, we must also analyze the quality of that debt.

There is nothing negative if a business or a country adds some leverage to conduct an investment that will generate a real economic return in the future. As some of those investments might fail due to unforeseen elements, the amount of debt taken must take into account the ability to repay it today, as well as the risks that the forecasted future revenues might be smaller.

The quality of debt is very important. Incurring into massive deficits to pay for current unproductive expenses means a higher burden in the future.

In my book, *Life In The Financial Markets,*[2] I mention the following items to understand the current danger:

---

[2] *Life In The Financial Markets.* Daniel Lacalle, Wiley, 2014.

The overindulgence of debt accumulation: The saturation threshold, destructive debt, and volatile cost of debt.

- The Threshold of Debt Saturation is the point at which an additional unit of debt does not generate economic growth, but simply causes further stagnation of the economy. This threshold was surpassed in the OECD, between 2005 and 2007.
- Destructive debt is the one generated by unproductive expenditure, which produces no positive effect on growth and perpetuates a system that confiscates and engulfs the real economy through taxes, detracting investment and annihilating consumption.
- Volatile cost of debt: As yields cannot be kept artificially low forever, we face the risk of debt shocks, because the outstanding debt increases while low yields are unsustainable.

"Cheap" debt tends to attract capital to low-productivity and short-term investments and leads to poor capital allocation.

If an investment is sound and in high-productivity sectors with strong value added, it will be profitable at a rate of 5 percent or 1 percent. Businesses that require high leverage and cheap rates tend to be extremely poor and risky. Furthermore, the constant push to "lend" because rates are low also leads to poor decision making. It is not a coincidence that the investments that thrive in credit booms are construction, real estate, ultra-leveraged bets, and short-term liquid financial assets. It is because they are the easiest sectors to deploy large sums of capital for a short-term profit.

The reality of the current environment is that, as the world has been approaching the limits of debt saturation, two things have happened.

First, recoveries are weaker (see Figure 7.2).

Second, overcapacity is perpetuated, as shown in Figure 7.3.

Without the cleansing factor of creative destruction in the excesses created in the economy, the burden of overcapacity takes hold of the economy and creates slack and lower growth. Even more importantly, overcapacity makes real productive investment stall, and the impact is felt in many areas of the economy.

For example, it is no coincidence that nonperforming loans have risen in European countries and Japan at the same time as liquidity and low interest

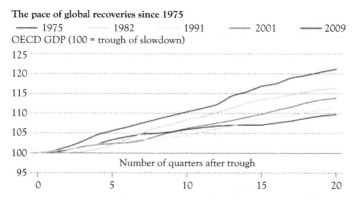

Figure 7.2 The pace of recoveries since 1975

Source: The Wall Street Journal; OECD.

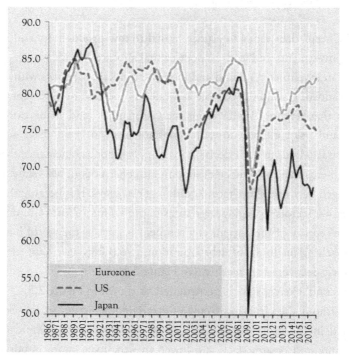

Figure 7.3 Capacity utilization in key economies

Source: World Bank; BIS.

rates took hold. Banks were unwilling to let companies go bankrupt and would help refinance any project they could in order to make it survive, thinking that maybe things would improve in a couple of years, or that lower interest rates would make the projects viable. None of the two things happened. But the other thing that did not happen was to let high-productivity sectors thrive.

The reality is that stimulus and government industrial plans are always directed at low-productivity, highly capital-intensive projects whose need is more than questionable. But these projects create "cheap and quick GDP" and give the impression of supporting jobs. Cheap debt multiplies that effect and at the same time erodes potential GDP.

Technology Does Not Kill Jobs

Meanwhile, mainstream media promotes the idea that technology kills jobs and that old economy industrial plans are what is needed, even though empirical evidence shows the contrary.

If technology destroyed jobs, there would be no jobs today, after the most dramatic evolution in technology seen at exponential pace in the past decades.

The evidence of more than 140 years shows that technology has created more jobs than it has destroyed. Study of census results in England and Wales since 1871 finds rise of machines has created jobs rather than making working humans obsolete.[3]

Technology helps create high-value-added jobs and at the same time destroys those that we do not want in the first place.[4]

Tax Burden Rises

But the mainstream message is oriented toward making us think that unemployment is due to globalization, world trade, technology, or any other force except the obvious: misallocation of capital into low-growth, poor return sectors and massive increase in taxation.

---

[3] Deloitte, 2016. Stewart, Debapratim De, and Alex Cole.
[4] www.theguardian.com/business/2015/aug/17/technology-created-more-jobs-than-destroyed-140-years-data-census

Country[1]	Total Tax wedge 2015	Annual change 2015/10 (in percentage points)[2]			
		Tax wedge	Income tax	Employee SSC	Employer SSC[3]
	(1)	(2)	(3)	(4)	(5)
Belgium	55.3	−0.62	−0.47	0.02	−0.18
Austria	49.5	1.34	1.44	0.02	−0.12
Germany	49.4	0.39	0.39	0.00	0.00
Hungary	49.0	2.42	1.25	1.17	0.00
Italy	49.0	1.79	1.79	0.00	0.00
France	48.5	−1.44	0.86	0.79	−3.09
Finland	43.9	1.59	0.17	0.91	0.50
Czech Republic	42.8	0.62	0.62	0.00	0.00
Sweden	42.7	−0.05	−0.05	0.00	0.00
Slovenia	42.6	0.04	0.04	0.00	0.00
Portugal	42.1	4.93	4.93	0.00	0.00
Slovak Republic	41.3	3.43	0.81	−0.40	3.02
Spain	39.6	−0.19	−0.19	0.00	0.00
Greece	39.3	−0.81	1.44	−0.05	−2.19
Estonia	39.0	−1.06	0.16	−0.89	−0.33
Turkey	38.3	1.33	0.71	−0.11	0.73
Luxembourg	38.3	3.95	2.89	0.46	0.60
Norway	36.6	−0.65	−1.15	0.34	0.16
Denmark	36.4	0.04	−0.17	0.00	0.10
Netherlands	36.2	−1.91	0.52	−1.94	−0.49
Poland	34.7	1.78	0.55	−0.27	1.49
Iceland	34.0	0.66	1.78	−0.12	−0.99
Japan	32.2	1.99	0.00	1.01	0.99
United States	31.7	0.91	0.96	0.00	−0.04
Canada	31.6	1.21	0.49	0.29	0.44
United Kingdom	30.8	−1.76	−1.91	0.13	0.02
Australia	28.4	1.52	1.74	0.00	−0.22
Ireland	27.5	1.65	0.91	0.74	0.00
Switzerland	22.2	0.12	−0.23	0.18	0.18
Korea	21.9	1.75	0.83	0.51	0.41

Israel	21.6	0.84	0.30	–0.12	0.66
Mexico	19.7	3.74	3.75	0.00	0.00
New Zealand	17.6	0.57	0.57	0.00	0.00
Chile	7.0	0.00	0.00	0.00	0.00
OECD	35.9	0.89	0.76	0.08	0.05

Source: OECD Note: Single individual without children at the income level of the average worker.

[1] Countries ranked by decreasing total tax wedge.

[2] Due to rounding, the changes in tax wedge in column (2) may differ by one tenth of percentage point from the sum of columns (3)–(5). For Denmark, the Green Check (cash benefit) contributes to the difference as it is not included in columns (3)–(5).

[3] Includes payroll taxes where applicable.

[4] The statistical data for Israel are supplied by and under the responsibility of the relevant Israeli authorities. The use of such data by the OECD is without prejudice to the status of the Golan Heights, East Jerusalem, and Israeli settlements in the West Bank under the terms of international law.

This change in the tax burden is essential to understand microeconomic effects and why the models that assume increases in consumption from lower rates and higher liquidity have been so wrong.

Cost of Capital Rises

We have mentioned in chapter 1, and throughout the book, that overcapacity and uncertainty reduce the desire of companies to invest despite massive liquidity and low rates.

And we mentioned that cost of capital does not fall. We need to understand this.

A company decides to invest in a project when the expected return on invested capital (ROIC) is higher than the weighted average cost of capital (WACC). This means that the company is making an economic real return over its cost of running the business.

This WACC is the weighted average of the cost of debt—which falls with low rates and high liquidity—and the cost of equity. What is this cost of equity? A firm's cost of equity represents the compensation the

Equity risk premia, %

Figure 7.4 Equity risk premia 1990–2016

Source: Citi; FactSet.

market demands in exchange for owning the asset and bearing the risk of ownership.[5]

One of the things that has happened in this period of massive financial repression, and is a driving factor behind the decision of companies to invest less despite low interest rates, is that the cost of equity has soared driven by the Equity Risk Premium. See Figure 7.4.

What does this mean? That although debt is cheap, equity is at 50-year highs in risk. It is more expensive, and therefore, the weighted cost of capital has not fallen, it has risen.

How can the cost of equity rise with massive liquidity? Because investors globally understand that the company's decision to invest one dollar of its cash in business growth is not attractive enough. Maybe the market does not understand overcapacity and tax burden, but understands that the likelihood of getting a positive return on new investments is poor, and that the risk is rising.

The reader might think this is simply a speculator's measure and that historically investors always prefer companies to stay put than to invest and expand. But that is incorrect. Investors had historically rewarded

---

[5] Investopedia.

sound expansion plans and ambitious growth projects. It is only since debt saturation was evident and becoming increasingly clear and stimulus plan after plan did not generate the expected growth that the market started to increase equity risk premia.

The reader might also think that this does not bother governments, who do not need to explain to investors in a General Shareholders' Meeting if investments have generated profits. But governments have a similar risk, and it is embedded in their relative cost of debt compared to the lowest-risk asset. Bond yield premiums and access to markets. Even if the entire debt was monetized, currency devaluation and mass inflation are the "cost of equity" of poor capital allocation of governments. The difference is that in the case of countries, it is the citizens that pay for their leaders' reckless actions.

Productive investment is not low relative to the solvent capital demand, but with respect to estimates of what is considered "normal" by mainstream economists and governments, which use as reference a bubble period.

The investment-to-savings ratio used by some central banks is fallacious because it ignores overcapacity, the level of indebtedness of the real economy, and technology, and above all because the "reference" was an abnormal period of excess.

Zombification of the economy. A weakening growth environment with a rising debt. The result: a massive amount of debt-financed, no-return spending that burdens and suffocates any productivity improvement.

Real negative rates destroy long-term investment and credit to the real economy, because they incentivize bubble-type short-term investment and investment in financial risky assets. Also the problems in the financial system rise as lending happens with rates disconnected with reality and real risk. Ken Garbade and Jamie McAndrews already alerted in 2012 of the negative effects of interest rates below zero.[6]

Low level of investment is not an anomaly; it is an evident and growing sign that overcapacity and excess debt are a global problem and that the real growth generated is very poor. Also, that "investment" without real economic profitability translates into white elephants (plans to build

---

[6] If Interest Rates Go Negative … Or, Be Careful What You Wish For, 2012.

things simply for the sake of building), more taxes, and more debt. And the velocity of money collapses. The economy is zombified.

Governments do not have better information or better skills than the private sector to identify attractive investments. But they do have the incentive of spending without worrying about the consequences and receiving no real penalty for it.

It is one thing to use leverage to grow and another to add debt to maintain GDP artificially.

The multiplier effect of public spending is inexistent in open and indebted economies.[7] Nobel laureate Angus Deaton names what is called the "Deaton paradox" which explains that the increase in public spending often generates the opposite effect. "Income shocks"—spending more—does not generate the desired "consumption shocks." Because the tax increases and the uncertainty created by the funnel effect in the real economy attack the marginal propensity to consume.

If governments carry out a number of investments without real economic return using surplus resources, it would not be a serious problem, but the mainstream Keynesian economists who seem only to follow Lord Maynard Keynes when thinking of spending and never to save and lower taxes, should have tattooed the words "to finance with deficits only investments with real economic returns."[8]

The world needs to recover supply-side policies, allow families and businesses to breathe, reduce taxes, and encourage productive investment by removing barriers to value-added sectors and eliminating subsidies to obsolete ones. But that does not provide photo opportunities or invitations to inaugurate bridges and airports.

Zombification. The engine of stagnation is to encourage wasteful spending and low-productivity investment in the hope that in the long run it will disguise itself. It confuses getting fat—sustaining GDP artificially—with getting stronger.

Repeating the same mistakes expecting different outcomes will not change this.

---

[7] Corsetti, Meier, and Müller, 2012, "Fiscal multipliers are negative in times of weakness in public finances."

[8] Collier and Brown "What Keynes Really Said About Deficit Spending."

PART II

How to Escape
the Monetary Tsunami

CHAPTER 8

When Commodities Collapse, Find A Hedge

"I used to make a phone call with a very thin dime, now I can't afford to even call to get the time"
> —Prince Charles and The City Beat Band

Many times, economic and financial market concepts seem really complicated and difficult to understand for the average citizen. However, if we have a discussion with friends in a bar or a restaurant, many understand the basic principles of commodities. And when we talk, we frequently debate on the challenges of supply and demand. Everybody more or less gets the idea of a finite resource and that price inflates when demand rises and reduces when supply is plentiful. On top of it, because we like conspiracy theories, we add assumptions of what producing countries' governments secretly think, what the real strategies in the global geopolitical landscape are, and how they affect pricing.

Commodities are much simpler than derivatives or equities.

The key to the definition of a commodity is that it is a basic resource which is used as a raw material for trade to exchange goods and services; as everyone understands the basic principles of their value, commodities many times work as money. However, commodities are used mainly as input to create a final product with higher value which will be sold at a profit.

It seems simple. But for financial markets, it is not. Commodities are also financial products, and have complicated structures that allow traders to buy and sell them as many times as needed. It is necessary for commodities to have a specified minimum standard, usually known in the market as basis grade.

Financial markets have broken down the historical barrier between producers and consumers of commodities by providing liquidity and flexibility. A large vessel carrying crude is bought and sold to different owners a few times in the course of the same trip from one port to another. Financial markets have diversified the uses and value of commodities and multiplied demand as these commodities became a trading opportunity and an investment. Transactions would not have to be physical, and millions of tons of any given commodity were traded in seconds.

Furthermore, the futures contracts exceed by many times the physical market.

Chris McMahon[1] explains it very well:

"Exchanges would always prefer cash settled over physical delivery because it is much easier. Physical delivery requires a tremendous amount of work.... It's a real nightmare.

For more than 100 years the basic premise of a futures contract was unchanged. It was a legally binding agreement to take, or to make, delivery of a prespecified quantity and quality of a commodity on a predetermined date at a predetermined location. By tying the futures contract to an actual, physically deliverable product, the integrity of the contract was backed up by underlying physical goods, ensuring that the market universally agreed to the fairness of the price. This allowed hedgers and speculators to more realistically take on and lay off the risk of production and purchase because the price of the futures contract would closely track the price of the physical commodity.

As contracts approach settlement, there are a series of notices to which traders must respond if they intend to take, or make, physical delivery. But most traders simply close out the positions by purchasing offsetting contracts.

By having the physical delivery aspect of the contract, it forces the prices to converge. That function forces cash and futures to be equal on that settlement day.

The exchange does not set the settlement prices. The settlement price of the physically delivered futures energy contracts is decided during the last 30 minutes of trading on the final trading day, and that price is used to determine margin calls and invoice prices for deliveries. In contrast, the cash settled

---

[1] Futures Magazine July 2006.

contracts settle on a futures price on the fourth business day before the 25th, hence the name 'penultimate,' and never go to delivery."

The reader may have heard numerous times that speculators and traders decide the price of a commodity by dealing on massive figures of financial instruments instead of buying and selling physical commodities. But that is not true; what they buy and sell are financial complex products linked to the price of the commodity in the physical market. The oil producer in Jeddah is not subject to the wave of speculation; that wave of speculation happens depending on what demand there is for the product in the physical market.

What Is the Price of Oil?

Or any commodity that trades in U.S. dollars, for that matter.

There is the nominal price and the real price. The first is what you discuss at dinnertime with friends and family. The second is the same price adjusted for inflation, caused by devaluation.

As all commodities trade in U.S. dollars, when the U.S. central bank devalues and increases money supply dramatically, commodities rise in nominal terms, not necessarily in real terms.

In fact, the casual dinnertime conversation about commodities and the fascinating conspiracy theories about geopolitical secret agendas are immediately killed by the real price argument. Bummer.

"Oil prices are at all-time high because of Saudi agendas, or conflicts, or China"… oops. Oil prices in real terms are at the same level as they were in 1978. Bummer.

Tim McMahon at InflationData.com[2] analyzes real and nominal prices for oil frequently. He states:

"Starting in 1946 the inflation adjusted price of oil was $18.03 per barrel. After climbing sharply for a couple of years, it stayed relatively steady and in fact steadily declined in inflation adjusted terms until 1973. From there prices exploded until 1980 when the bubble burst and prices returned to 'normal' however they were much more volatile from then on.

---

[2] Oil Prices in Inflation Adjusted Terms, October 2016, inflationdata.com

The major peaks occurred in December 1979 at $119.33, October 1990 at $62.59, and June 2008 at $139.05 (all inflation adjusted to 2016 dollars). Another interesting item to note is that the average price has been increasing. The average for the entire period from 1946 to present is $42.54."
"Adjusted for inflation the 1979 $38 peak oil price is the equivalent of paying $119.33 today (meaning Oct 2016)."

A real party breaker. Most of the stories about geopolitical conspiracies and the amazing science fiction theories about the end of oil (called peak oil) vanish when you understand that the vast majority of boom and bust shocks in the King of Commodities, crude, have been—yawn— monetary changes.

Hola, Mr. Fed

Yes, there have been price spikes due to fundamental aspects. Oil crises from OPEC cuts, supply affecting wars ... all of it is there. And in real terms oil has appreciated since 1980. But the big monsters in the room dictating price are called Mr. Federal Reserve and the mighty U.S. dollar.

Once you understand money supply as a deciding factor for commodity pricing, the complaints about speculators and evil manipulators disappear.

More importantly, once countries and central banks understand that it's the reserve currency and its effect that matters the most, it is easier to make a fundamental analysis of other real variables that affect the price, and whether those trends are sustainable or just mirages.

Unfortunately, many, even knowing this reality, make the mistake of believing that "this time it's different."

If countries had taken the tsunami of dollars generated by massive monetary manipulation for what it was—a mirage—it would have been much easier for them to understand the inevitable collapse when the seemingly endless flow of cheap dollars finished.

Preparing for a bubble is difficult. A rising wave of liquidity is very tempting and many people become very rich quickly. The perverse incentives to allow everyone to believe the trap are enormous.

Boom and Bust

The commodities boom and bubble was born before QE, but reached phenomenal heights with it. The fact that it started earlier does not mean it is not due to "expansionary policies." The commodities supercycle started at the beginning of the new millennium, just in time to fill the void created after the colossal tech-stock bubble burst of the1990s, with massive interest rate cuts to "stimulate the economy" and survive the bust of a bubble with a new—and seemingly more credible—one.

As Keith McCullough[3] always says: "There is a difference between a unicorn and a bubble. A bubble, at least for a short period of time, is something real, tangible. Unicorns don't exist." The tech bubble came from the belief in unicorns. The commodity bubble had a certain fundamental reality to it, at least for a while. To the tangible fundamentals, in order to fuel the bubble, the market added the "peak" concept. Consumption was so out of control that we would run out of oil, gas, and other commodities sooner than any substitution could appear. To justify that "bubble argument," the market added another bubble: the perennial and unstoppable growth of China.

Of course, all those bubble-justifying arguments were presented with tremendous "scientific" studies and alarmist conclusions. A great business for those involved. But all of them ignored reality. Cycles happen; efficiency is a bitch, and it erodes Excel spreadsheet demand models; technology leads to new discoveries and better and more diversified production.

The biggest enemy of a bubble estimate is an engineer.

Commodities had been in a steady bear market since the early 1980s and were virtually ignored by investors in favor of rapidly rising stocks. Energy products and precious metals started showing definite signs of life again in 1999, but the real commodities boom began in earnest in November 2001, just as the Federal Reserve's aggressive interest rate cuts aimed to stop the post–tech crash recession on its tracks.

Commodities prices, as measured by the Continuous Commodity Index (CCI), rose a staggering 275 percent since the start of their bull market in November 2001, against a 25 percent increase in overall inflation as measured by the CPI.

---

[3] Hedgeye CEO.

What is impressive about this commodities bull market is not just the magnitude of the price increases but also the sheer breadth of commodities involved, from Malaysian palm oil and rare earth metals to sulfuric acid and uranium, with virtually no commodity missing out on the bounty. Thank you, Federal Reserve.

While the global financial crisis of late 2008 resulted in a 48 percent plunge in commodity prices, they staged a quick and powerful recovery, rising 112 percent from the depths of the crisis to a mid-2011 peak that surpassed the prior 2008 high by over 10 percent.

A massive bubble, inflated by ultralow rates, burst and created a financial crisis, and the solution was to ... fuel the bubble again.

At this point, there is an important thing to say. Mainstream economics and most academia deny the existence of bubbles. However, there are relevant studies that analyze how they are created, almost invariably, from the perception of low risk, and the idea that valuations and fundamentals have changed to a new paradigm.[4] Some papers even find bubbles a great way to go from financial crises to growth, as if the crises were not generated by the bubbles themselves, and the exit is weaker growth.[5]

Like all bubbles, the commodity bubble of the 2000s started as a legitimate economic trend[6] and evolved into a "new paradigm"—the "fundamentals have changed" speculative mania.

A critical component of every bubble is a convincing underlying story with widely acceptable elements of truth to be believable not only in the minds of the otherwise intelligent and well-educated people who control market-moving amounts of capital ... but also of their clients, media, and analysts.

The elements of truth responsible for the justifiable or "nonbubble" portion of the commodities price boom were: underinvestment in natural resource productive capacity during the 1980s and 1990s; the 2000s' U.S. dollar bear market; the fundamental shift in the economy of

---

[4] Bubbles, Financial Crises, and Systemic Risk. Markus K. Brunnermeier, Martin Oehmke. Columbia. 2010.

[5] Economic Growth with Bubbles. Alberto Martin and Jaume Ventura. 2011.

[6] Bubbles, Rational Expectations and Financial Markets. Olivier J. Blanchard, Mark W. Watson, 1986.

China, India, and other emerging markets; population and middle-class growth; climate change and extreme weather; geopolitical turmoil; and the increased diversion of agricultural commodities for use in biofuels.

Some legitimate portion of the increase in commodities prices since 2001 can certainly be explained by the aforementioned fundamentals, but it is also important to realize that most were also exaggerated and magnified to adapt to the ever-rising price discourse. Furthermore, when some of those factors—supply, China, technology—ended being questioned, others would be further exaggerated. Peak oil worked wonders to help this and the "next year" fallacy we mentioned with hockey stick estimates.

"The only cure for high prices is ... high prices."[7]

As high prices eventually encourage more supply to enter the market, they push prices down again. And this supply comes to the market following the belief in endless growth in China, emerging markets, and so on.

Prices are viewed as a reflection of a reality and a future that is unquestionable, without discerning whether the price formation is following supply, demand, and inventories. One of the indicators that the bubble was exactly that, was the fact that supply kept rising and inventories building while demand growth estimates were revised down every few months between January predictions and December reality.

Record-high commodities prices led to ambitious investment plans, such as projects in Quebec and Canada's multibillion investment and the decision to open its vast Northern region to mining development—an area twice the size of France with an abundance of iron, nickel, and copper ore deposits. From Australia to Brazil, Russia to Madagascar, new and massive development projects went rapidly into Final Investment Decision (FID) and capex. China's growth and "endless thirst" for commodities justified even the most challenging of economics. Investments in resource exploration, mining, and development exceeded $1.5 trillion a year. Ten times more, in real terms, than historical averages.

Record food prices incentivized the planting of new farm fields, causing a global wheat supply glut to swell to its biggest in a decade. While the rise of China is commonly cited as a reason for rising food prices, China

---

[7] The Cure For High Prices Is ... High Prices—Leigh Drogen, Blog. 2011.

could meet its own demand for food and even become a significant food exporter. Chinese interests have also started to unlock Africa's abundant undeveloped agricultural potential using modern farming techniques.

Dollar Collapse, Commodity Boom, Then Bust

The strongest driver of the commodities bull market was the 40 percent decline in the U.S. dollar's exchange rate versus its basket of currencies since 2001.

The next main catalysts for the second phase of the commodities bubble (2009 to 2013) was the launch of the Federal Reserve's QE programs.

But by QE3, the third phase, the carry trade—"long commodities and short dollar"—was disappearing. Like all bubbles, the mirage of the exaggerated fundamentals was rapidly fading, and the reality of oversupply was becoming more evident.

Estimates of real demand started to come down aggressively, and with them the world GDP growth expectations. Supply kept rising and thousands of projects with questionable economics kept adding production because they became sunken costs and producers needed to generate cash, not returns over cost of capital.

The collapse in commodities was as quick as the rise, and its force came as a surprise even to the analysts and economists that predicted the burst of the bubble. I wrote *The Energy World Is Flat* in 2014 with the view that oil prices would fall from nearly $100 to half, and prices crashed to lows of $25–$30 a barrel.

Like the bubble, fundamentals were exaggerated and misunderstood. But after an entire generation of traders had been raised on the belief that commodities could only go up, the fall was more severe as few could discern real fundamental value as the bottom approached.

To find real value we must understand real monetary bubbles and money supply.

Those that analyzed the economy and the fundamentals of commodities understanding the peaks and bottoms of fundamental supply and demand cycles were able to pick great opportunities and, more importantly, avoid the magic ideas of new paradigms and endless inflation.

The opportunity that the end of the commodity supercycle provided was enormous, as long as governments, investors, traders, and citizens sobered up and understood that the analysis we had made for almost two decades was sugarcoated by the placebo effect of monetary policy.

We cannot just complain about these policies. They have been going on for centuries. There is always a government or a central bank that will believe that this time they will get away with inflating assets and destroying currencies with no consequence. But they always fail. We, as investors, economists, and analysts need to understand that these policies will create shorter and more abrupt cycles, be intelligent enough to ride them while the wave is rising, and be prudent enough not to believe what is simply unbelievable: that this time we have found the recipe to mitigate and offset any economic cycle. It is simply untrue.

CHAPTER 9

Twenty-Five Central Banks Easing, Lessons and Examples

"Like a full force gale, I was lifted up again"

—Van Morrison

What is a monetary tsunami?

The massive monetary stimulus created in the past decade is unprecedented.

The United States created more money between 2008 and 2016 than in its entire previous history,[1] and China multiplied its money supply by four. Broad money as a percentage of GDP globally exploded 20 percent in this period.[2]

Many monetarists believe that all of this is nonsense because a large part of this money is "sequestered" as excess reserves in the financial system. It does not matter, because those reserves fuel the liquid financial asset bubble and the imbalances of banks.

I call the consequences a monetary tsunami because it is formed in a similar way. A series of waves in a water body caused by the displacement of a large volume of water. A series of financial crises generating a domino effect.

The monetary tsunami happens when a) part of the massive amount of money is unleashed into the economy and b) the massive liquidity that is created to abort a financial crisis does not create any mitigating effect.

---

[1] St. Louis adjusted monetary base: US$874.82 billion by 2008. Multiplied to US$3,418.37 billion by January 2017.

[2] World Bank data.

When this happens, it will not matter if mainstream blames banks, or speculators—believe me, they will—or calls for even more aggressive monetary stimulus. Because all of it *will* happen. But the reader is interested in escaping from the inevitable consequences, not in finding an easy scapegoat.

Looking for a scapegoat is essential in out-of-control monetary policies. In the French Revolution, the authorities blamed shop owners for not willing to accept Assignats, the useless currency that flooded the country. In Venezuela, they blamed an economic war and even used an excuse that speculators were hoarding cash notes in Poland, forgetting that if that were the case, the currency would revalue, not devalue. In Spain, in 2008, the media and the government blamed hedge funds. There is always a scapegoat to justify the excesses of the past and deny its consequences.

The Biggest Risk: The Energy and Food Burden

What creates inflation is monetary policy at the end of the day.
—Robert Plosser[3]

The most important risk is that by trying desperately and with more aggressive measures to create inflation, you may succeed. Too much, too quickly, and negatively.

This would be my worst-case scenario: out-of-control inflation in commodities—food and energy—while core CPI remains subdued due to the slack in the economies, large debt, and overcapacity.

This scenario would lead quickly to a 2008-type crisis. Commodities would rise well above supply and demand logic, and the oil burden—the amount of GDP that the OECD consumes in crude—would exceed 10 percent. See Figure 9.1.

The oil burden, in my view, is a bad economic term more oriented to the old, heavily industrialized economies. Throughout the past decades, when OECD economies spent around 4 percent of GDP in oil, it was an almost certain risk of an imminent crisis. Families and industries would

---

[3] March 25, 2011.

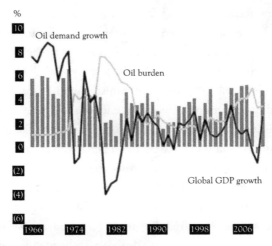

Figure 9.1 Oil burden and GDP impact

Source: World Bank.

be unable to sustain the rising costs, loans in different sectors would be at risk, and the financial system would suffer a shock from nonperforming loans and slowdown of the energy-importing economies.

This measure has always been used by debunked peak oil theorists to alert of the end of oil supply and the impending doom of depleting reserves, but it is simply a monetary effect. Too much money supply makes commodities—denominated and traded in dollars—rise when the U.S. currency is debased artificially.

It is not just the burden as a percentage of GDP that matters, but the severity and speed of the rise. Economies face enormous difficulties adapting to an environment where prices in foreign currency are rising faster than the ability to undertake emergency policies. This unexpected and abrupt burst of inflation does not translate into higher wages or more productivity; it just loads the economy with a rising cost that is not generating growth; it stagnates the economy.

The reader might think that this effect is only on the importing countries, but at the same time the producers thrive. And you would be right. And that is why I dislike the oil burden alone as a concept of rising risk and why I prefer the "energy and food burden." Because, as we saw in past oil crises that had an unquestionable monetary origin, the producing countries witness an unprecedented rise in food prices. This leads to either a heavier burden of subsidies on the government or massive difficulties for the population, suffering from an inflation that is not covered by their meager wages.

We must consider this because it is quite typical that, when energy prices rise, media and consensus economists mention the positive effect on commodity-rich countries without understanding the impact of rising food prices. According to the World Bank, the average of household income spent on food is close to 35 to 40 percent in these countries.[4] So, no, producers do not benefit from rising commodities as much as some think, particularly when such rise is quick and dramatic. The reader might think that all of this is fine but energy commodities can go up much more than food. Difficult. As a friend of mine always says, "We eat energy." Many of the costs of energy commodities are embedded in food prices.

That is why I would use the "food and energy chain burden." The amount of oil required for a unit of GDP, that is, the oil intensity of economies, has dropped dramatically in the past decades, and oil alone does not explain the risk of a shock. But a monetary policy-based rapid shock in energy and food commodities would be a much more precise measure of a coming financial crisis. It is safe to assume that when this "burden" surpasses 5 percent of world GDP we should be quite concerned.

How do a country and its citizens escape this shock?

First, using periods of low prices to invest in technology and substitutes. A country that is able to have a competitive and diversified primary energy use has a double advantage: lower cost of imports and higher flexibility. Investing in agriculture technology and improving productivity reduce the shocks of energy prices and secure supply, added to a balanced combination of genetically modified food and organic supply.

Producing countries need to increase investment in water management and agriculture technology and diversify their economies from commodities using the extraordinary revenues of boom periods to strengthen the economy for the next crisis, instead of wasteful spend in useless megalomaniac infrastructure projects.

Furthermore, periods of excess revenues should be used to reduce debt and avoid a sudden stop when cheap dollars stop arriving.

---

[4] http://wsm.wsu.edu/researcher/wsmaug11_billions.pdf

That was the difference between Saudi Arabia and Venezuela during the commodity boom. Saudi Arabia reduced debt from an average of 38.5 percent to an all-time low of 1.6 percent in 2014, which allowed the country to take large deficits to finance the expenditures of the government when oil prices collapsed. In the case of Venezuela, the country wasted more than $300 billion of extraordinary revenues and found itself with constantly diminishing foreign currency reserves and massive inflation when oil prices fell. Adding insult to injury, the policy of nationalizing thousands of companies left the country crippled with poorly run expropriated firms that ended bankrupt or with the lowest production levels in nearly a decade.

Additionally, taking measures to guarantee ample foreign exchange reserves and monitor excess borrowing in households and industries is critical. Recognizing that cycles become shorter and that the impact of a monetary and economic crisis will be felt for many years is an essential part of prudent governance. But admitting, after decades, that infrastructure spending must be adequately analyzed so that it does not become a weight on the economy's potential growth is also essential.

Let us think of the consumer nations. Developed countries have a much better set of tools to respond to a commodity shock. But they also are ill-prepared for financial shocks that tend to follow them. Even more worrisome, developed nations are the first ones to fall in the trap of believing the exponential growth and the mirage of emerging market wealth even when it is coming from their own expansionary policies.

What happens is that most of the credit to finance the white elephants and excess spend of emerging markets is originated in developed nations. When a shock as the one described happens, capital in financial institutions falls dramatically. The impact on nonperforming loans affects credit to domestic companies and families as well; imbalances are generated by those same companies that believed in the mirage and overinvested in risky economies looking for growth and inflation.

Sometimes, Banks Do Well

This risk was adequately contained in the high-yield energy crisis in 2014 and 2015.

Energy companies had seen unprecedented access to debt markets throughout the boom in commodities created by the Federal Reserve and could finance capex and growth with cheap funding. In 2005 energy was around 4.5 percent of the high-yield market, that is, the bonds with higher risk and higher returns. By 2014, energy had risen to 15 percent.[5]

Despite some media and consensus commentators calling for an equivalent of the housing bubble, it did not happen.

Banks were very worried about the rising risk in energy many years before the peak in high-yield bonds. As such, syndications, by which banks reduce risk sharing it with many others, were the norm. Furthermore, unlike housing before the crisis, these asset-backed loans were also supported by a healthy level of mergers and acquisition transactions that ensured a minimum valuation existed. These loans were not worth zero.

Of the total high-yield debt of the United States, less than 15 percent was in energy and that included solar investments. Of the total investment-grade debt, less than 10 percent was in energy—including electricity. The fact that more than 89 percent of the country's production was in large companies with little debt ensured that any crisis would trigger an asset transaction boom from predators' bargain hunting.

Therefore, even if the market could consider that 25 percent of that debt was "unpayable," the impact on the economy and the sector would be very small.

Deutsche Bank showed in a 2016 report (*Should the Fed worry about the energy sector?*) that the rate of default had not exceeded 5 percent. It was between 9 and 14 percent from 2008 to 2009.

Of the 120 companies that concentrated 95 percent of U.S. oil production, 97 have less than 1.6x debt over EBITDA[6] and 79, less than 0.6x. More than $90 billion capital increases had been implemented. Despite the rise in risk, it was nothing like the housing bubble.

This fear of repeating a similar concentration of risk led to a completely different outcome. Yes, many small inefficient energy companies defaulted, and the spread at which the riskier names borrowed relative to investment grade soared … but the domino effect created by the subprime crisis did not result in a financial and economic collapse.

---

[5] Source: Simmons.

[6] Earnings Before Interest, Taxes, Depreciation, and Amortization.

Lesson learned? Not really. A lot of these risks were simply disguised by the increased excess liquidity generated by central banks. But the period from 2014 to 2016 showed to us that despite the many challenges in emerging markets, energy, and European banks, none of those events resulted in a massive financial crisis.

The Impressive Example of the Russian Central Bank

Twenty-five central banks in the world undertook aggressive measures to boost growth. The main tools, obviously, were to lower interest rates and devalue. The result, even more obviously, was that growth did not improve and financial repression simply weakened consumption and debt repayment ability.

It is called beggar-thy-neighbor policy because the idea is to devalue the currency, boost competitiveness, and increase exports, and all of it at the expense of the country to which we intend to sell our goods and services. What a great idea. To profit from our trading partners by creating massive imbalances in our economy.

Devaluation, as we said, is nothing but a hidden subsidy to crony sectors at the expense of savers. But sometimes devaluation is simply the process of reckoning of a previous exuberance in the currency and an excess that comes to an end.

There is one central bank in the world that refused to sugarcoat the economy's imbalances with monetary laughing gas. Russia, of all places.

The governor, Elvira Nabiullina, did not fall in the trap of lowering interest rates and printing money to try to boost investment no matter what. Her policies were to closely monitor perverse incentives, penalize banks for not dealing with nonperforming loans, make very mild adjustments to interest rates, and allow the economy to adapt to a lower oil price and different macroeconomic environment without inflating financial asset bubbles. Many market participants criticized her for implementing a "tough love" monetary policy that was completely against the trend of central banks all over Latin America and the OECD.

While others expanded their balance sheet dramatically,[7] buying sovereign and asset-backed securities, the Russian central bank's assets were adding precious metals and deposits, and the size of the balance sheet was a fraction, relative to GDP, of that of any of the OECD counterparts. Rates remained high and liquidity contained, placing the policy of maintaining strong foreign currency reserves and gold at the forefront, relative to defending financial asset valuations. The vast majority of the Russian budget is in rubles. This allowed the country to reduce debt and maintain its spending in local terms—despite a devaluation that came from lower oil prices and external sanctions—and a level of inflation that the central bank recognized as part of the fundamentals of the economy and that was adequately covered by wages.

And Nabiullina was right. Monetary policy did not become a conduit for excess leverage and massive asset bubbles. Yes, markets dropped, and the government spending was contained in real terms. But the economy strengthened because it was better prepared for the difficult period by not denying reality, and by the time oil prices—the most important source of export revenues for the country—and sanctions were to be lifted, the economy would be much healthier.

In an interview, she explained:[8]

> The first thing we see is that the key limiting factor for investment is not so much our high rate and tough monetary policy but rather structural limitations, the state of the investment climate and so on and so forth. Therefore, we believe that through our rate decision we will not be reducing economic growth and that the problems of economic growth have their root in structural limitations. In addition, our country's economy will have to learn to live with a background of a really positive interest rate. This means that we will need investment into the improvement of labor productivity, we will need to improve efficiency and reduce costs, and this is precisely the kind of signal that our monetary policy is sending to the market.

---

[7] A comparative analysis of developments in central bank balance sheet composition. Christiaan Pattipeilohy.

[8] Friday, 23 Sep 2016, CNBC.

By 2016, when oil prices had stabilized and the imbalances of the Russian economy had been largely contained, the governor of the central bank could be very proud to be one of the very few commodity producers that did not damage the long-term growth potential of the economy by betting on monetary policy to disguise reality or promote taking massive amounts of debt that would result in a burden for future generations.

Thanks to the Russian central bank's policy, the country did not have to increase tax rates—Russia is one of the most attractive tax regimes in the world, with a low flat tax—to pay for the excess of debt that would have been accumulated by the government if it had followed the "example" of other central banks. Thanks to this "tough love" policy and a very tight and inflexible leash on risky lending, the country did not have to bail out overleveraged financial entities.

The reality is that Elvira Nabiullina and her team followed an almost Austrian approach to monetary policy: Recognize that cycles exist. She did not try to fool markets or the government by thinking that lowering rates and exploding liquidity would boost investment, because she made an absolutely spot-on analysis of structural strengths and challenges. Her goal was not to boost GDP artificially or fool anyone with the "wealth effect" by inflating asset prices. Her goal was to help the economy endure the pain of a recessive cycle without harming the economy further. And she succeeded. To me, the policy of the Russian central bank during the sudden stop in emerging markets was exemplary of what needs to be done to come out of a difficult period stronger and equipped with plenty of policy tools to manage any forthcoming challenge.

The lessons that emerging and developed economies could learn from the Russian central bank are plenty: Do not deny cycles, avoid science fiction guidance, implement a policy that recognizes the structural issues without trying to disguise them and, most of all, reject leaving a massive burden of debt and financial bubbles to future generations just to perpetuate the mistakes of the past.

Bravo, Elvira. Not many Keynesian consensus economists and bankers will recognize your excellent analysis and policies, but your country and its citizens clearly feel stronger.

The Russian was one that did not fall in the Central Bank Trap.

CHAPTER 10

Lessons for Central Banks. Secular Stagnation and Fiscal Multipliers

"And then the harder they come, the harder they fall, one and all"
—Jimmy Cliff

We have analyzed many key elements of the failure of the central bank trap. Let us summarize a few:

- Creating bubbles that need to be maintained afterward to avoid a financial crisis
- Trying to solve a problem of debt with more debt
- Assuming investment and growth are weak because of a demand problem, not a structural issue
- Generating collateral damages in emerging markets and commodities

In the recent times, we have witnessed another, and worrying, side effect. The reaction from voters against the establishment becomes more aggressive as citizens do perceive that all those massive stimuli do not get to them.

We have also mentioned a few actions that have worked.

But the main economies' central banks need to take measures to address their rapidly declining credibility.

Let us start with a few recommendations.

Won't Get Fooled Again

One of the main mistakes of central banks is to provide extremely detailed forecasts that are met rarely or never.

In chapter 3, where we discussed the hockey stick mistake, we showed that the discrepancy between the estimated impact of monetary policy and reality has sometimes been 100 percent.

Central bankers have plenty of excuses to justify these mistakes, but the reality is that investors, companies, and families do not believe in these estimates anymore.

Furthermore, as we have seen with opinion polls, it reaches a point where the impact is actually the opposite of what is expected.

So, the first solution is for central banks to provide stricter guidance with more complex sensitivities.

Bernanke's famous quote that monetary policy is 98 percent communication and 2 percent action is true. When there is credibility. If the market and economic agents see the central banks lose credibility, it will not matter. Neither the action nor the communication will work.

Guidance should not be about macroeconomic aggregates like GDP or rate of unemployment, let alone inflation. It should be about what money is actually all about, short-term credit, and benefits for SMEs, and this guidance should be monitored on a monthly basis.

Consistency and credibility in guidance is essential.

Scrap big headlines about GDP and employment. Those are second derivatives, at best, of monetary policy.

By trying to show that the policy is only about main street instead of helping the transition for financial entities, central banks have destroyed their credibility.

Central banks will regain credibility when they show the benefits of monetary policy by focusing the main headlines on the transmission mechanism of its actions.

Citizens can understand the short-term benefits of improved lending to SMEs or, the most important headline of them all, the actions taken to strengthen banks without hurting the real economy.

But, most importantly, central banks must avoid providing messages to "appease" financial markets.

If a central bank is to succeed in delivering a credible message to main street, it cannot just give empty talk of main street.

The average citizen is not stupid. They know that central banks end up catering to Wall Street by the market reaction.

Let us face it. Saying that buying bonds creates employment is like saying that if we all dance together, it will rain.

Central bank managers that might read this book will likely say that all the things that I mentioned are in the extremely detailed reports they make. And they will be missing the point.

One can make a 100-page report stating numerous factors about monetary policy, but they are denying the fact that estimates have been the driving force of the message to society, and central banks have lost their credibility by missing their own projections over and over. I come back to Paul Romer's excellent piece.[1]

I know it is not the intention of the staff or management of central banks to lose credibility and make mistakes in predictions, the same way as it is not an analyst's intention to overestimate earnings. But failing to understand that in the process, they are losing credibility, and that this is something exceptionally dangerous for central banks, is a big risk.

The entire status of a currency as global reserve depends on the credibility of its economic policies and its central bank.

As such, it is imperative that forecasting is focused exclusively on the elements in which central banks' staff have a clear evidence of correlation and causation.

It is imperative that central banks use sensitivities in their analysis.

It is also essential that guidance is clear and the basic assumptions behind that guidance are provided upfront and in detail. There is a reason why the average citizens dismiss central banks as alchemists. There isn't only two factors that affect the real economy. Interest rates and money supply are simply just two elements, but there are many more. Ignoring aging, overcapacity, tax burden, and so many other factors is dangerous because it puts the attention on the central bank as a failure, and governments sit back happily blaming monetary policy for their inaction.

There is a strong improvement and credibility in the words of some of the central banks recently—they are being less simplistic and focusing more on structural aspects—but I cannot stress enough the importance

---

[1] The Trouble with Macroeconomics. Paul Romer, Stern School of Business, New York University. September, 2016.

of managing communication and guidance in a much more realistic way, and being realistic is also recognizing risks in financial assets.

Denying bubbles tops the list of central banks' "problems." How can an average investor or citizen trust in the biggest experts in finance and economics if they are unable to recognize, sometimes even justify, evident exuberance in financial markets?

The entire communication and guidance policy of central banks needs to change. Focus on those points where causation is real, not on justifying the reason why it does not happen afterward. Forget alchemist messages.

Draghi has changed communication policy by constantly referring to structural reforms, downside risks, and fundamental elements. This, in turn, has been one of the reasons—apart from poor earnings—why European stock markets have not been as insanely overoptimistic in their reaction as others. But there are relevant elements of improvement, particularly in sovereign debt. Showing governments the risk of adding more debt if interest rises is completely absent from big headlines, and it is an enormous factor of instability.

The ECB, for example, should present the impact of a 1 percent rise in rates on interest payment and government deficits and make it abundantly clear to voters ahead of promises of more spending and the inevitable end of QE.

Credibility-enhancing communication is a critical factor. It will help citizens understand the actions and, more importantly, help avoid an enraged crowd of voters from thinking that they are being swindled and robbed leading them to vote for radical defenders of magical solutions.

The purpose of a central bank is to help mitigate the impact of the process of solving imbalances on the economy, not to perpetuate those imbalances.

No Romance Without Finance

There is a way of avoiding—or at least minimizing—the accumulation of risk in financial assets. No, it is not ending central banks or going back to the gold standard or similar, which, in the current world of massive debt, would be impossible to implement, because even if one country did it, the others in the currency reserve system would likely fail to follow suit.

Expanding without control the balance sheet of the central bank. We are told every day by many that it has no negative consequences because there is no inflation ... except, there is. Massive inflation in financial assets. Furthermore, inflation expectations were already rising fast in 2016, and the BoJ, the ECB, and many other central banks continued expanding their balance sheet as if nothing happened.

Monetization of debt and hiding bonds under the central bank carpet is exactly the same as any other form of excessive risk-taking. And the bubble in bonds is simply spectacular.

> In the modern economy, most money takes the form of bank deposits. But how those bank deposits are created is often misunderstood: the principal way is through commercial banks making loans. Whenever a bank makes a loan, it simultaneously creates a matching deposit in the borrower's bank account, thereby creating new money.
>
> The reality of how money is created today differs from the description found in some economics textbooks:
>
> • Rather than banks receiving deposits when households save and then lending them out, bank lending creates deposits.
> • In normal times, the central bank does not fix the amount of money in circulation, nor is central bank money "multiplied up" into more loans and deposits.
>
> Although commercial banks create money through lending, they cannot do so freely without limit.[2]

Herein lies the solution.

On one side, central banks should monitor money supply and credit growth relative to the real GDP. If money supply exceeds five-year historical real GDP growth, it would be a first signal of excess. But it needs to be more complex. Money supply and credit growth must also be analyzed in their quality. A proper analysis of the sectors and areas where the accumulation of credit occurs and the price increases in such asset or sector

---

[2] Money creation in the modern economy. Michael McLeay, Amar Radia, and Ryland Thomas. Monetary Analysis Directorate, 2014.

should be adequately monitored as well, not to justify abnormal rises in prices as a "new paradigm" but as a measure of risk.

In fact, central banks should have a cascade of red and green lights when analyzing the increase in money supply.

First, price signals in bonds and risky assets versus its fundamentals.

Central banks can monitor the improvement in debt repayment ability and there is plenty of data coming from rating agencies.

When lending rises, yields fall, and there is a simultaneous underlying trend of worsening solvency and liquidity, the central bank must take action to avoid a bubble.

Lowering interest rates can only be a measure that helps the economy if there is an undoubted discrepancy between the real risk and the market. For example, one can argue that the euro crisis created a disproportionate risk based on concerns that the single currency would break up. This is an anomaly, or at least it can cause panic. The solution might entail lowering interest rates but at the end of the day is just a matter of confidence. In that case, Mario Draghi did more for Europe's stability saying the famous words, "We will do whatever it takes and it will be enough,"[3] than purchasing €80 billion a month of government bonds while building a trillion in excess liquidity.

Additionally, central banks should analyze investment and credit growth trends using larger historical periods in order to avoid making estimates of excess or lack of investment looking at a period of time that was clearly an anomaly. If central banks look at investment to savings in a 20-year period instead of the past five years, their analysis of "too much" or "too little" savings varies enormously.

Therefore, the main characteristic of a prudent monetary policy should be to change the objective. Price stability is important, but inflation for inflation's sake should not be.

To avoid money supply growing more than real GDP greatly reduces the risk of bubbles. Monitoring real causation between interest rates and investment does the same. Lowering interest rates for the sake of it is a recipe for bubbles.

---

[3] July 26, 2012.

Table 10.1 Schematic representation of risk in negative rates

Frictions					Risks
Lowering the repo rate to	Deposit rate (households)	Lending rate	Interest rate channel	Cash is profitable	Additional stability risks at different levels of the repo rate
Weakly negative	Does not follow	Follows	OK	No	Exaggerated risk-taking
		Partially follows	Weak	For some	FRN, reallocation of deposits
		Does not follow	Very weak	For many	
Very negative	Follows	Follows	Weak	For most	Liquidity risks for banks

Source: BNP.

The central bank should understand that if a company's decision to undertake an investment did not happen at 1 percent rates, it will not happen at 0.5 percent either.

In fact, governments and central banks should understand that if a company's investment is not viable at 1 percent and it becomes viable at 0.5 percent, it is not just a massively dangerous investment, but a guarantee of failure.

The law of diminishing returns with interest-rate cuts is pretty evident after more than 600 of them. Believing that negative real interest rates would change that negative spiral is delusional. See Table 10.1.

Negative real interest rates, as we mentioned before, encourage short-term risky lending in liquid financial assets and discourage long-term real economy lending.

If central banks monitor these variables properly and forget about aggregate data and objectives where monetary policy offers no causation, the risks we have outlined throughout this book would be mitigated significantly.

A close monitor of quality and accumulation of credit by asset and sector.

A more robust analysis of valuation of risky assets and bonds.

A better understanding of the transmission mechanism, recognizing structural issues outside of cost and availability of credit (overcapacity, real demand).

When understanding the role of a central bank, it should be both to help break unnecessary panics and to attack unjustified euphoria. The latter is as dangerous as the former.

Break All The Rules?

Credit growth is important if it is productive debt. Therefore, regulation of the financial system must be simpler and more focused on quality than on perverse incentives.

Excess regulation is as bad as no regulation. It leads to the same perverse incentives. Excessive imbalances.

The central bank should try to avoid trusting credit growth as the only metric without understanding what it is comprised of.

Regulation needs to be simple and effective.

Most of the excess in regulation we have seen in the past years comes from trying to protect the system from the last crisis, not the next one.

Regulators all over the world are generating millions of pages of rules to avoid 2008, not the current flow of imbalances.

The main reason why regulation tends to fail is because governments and regulators confuse quantity—lots of reports and filings—with quality.

The other fundamental reason is that regulation tends to incentivize excess risk—taking in assets that are perceived as low-risk by the same regulators—and that is where the next crisis will come from.

Take the EU, where the founding papers and the entire banking regulation were based on the principle that government bonds had zero risk. In the rules they hid the time bomb.

Producing hundreds of pages of new rules every week just does not work.

Monitoring accumulation and quality of loans does.

For example, the EU will always have more trouble getting out of crises and seeing their banks solve their imbalances because loans are valued at a combination of market value and mark-to-model.

What does this mean? That banks may account assets in their books at a much higher valuation than what the market would pay for those assets under the justification that it is a very short-term metric and that they have done extensive research to prove that the book value of those assets is much higher than what market transactions would dictate.

No wonder that European banks have been, at the end of 2016, slower and less effective at dealing with the crisis.

No wonder, either, that European banks trade at a massive discount in price to book value relative to their U.S. counterparts. Very few believe the "book value."

Yes, having constant mark-to-market, as U.S. banks do, may create short-term pain when markets fall, but it also helps the entities to be in touch with reality, to avoid accumulating nonperforming loans and refinancing them forever, and to take more aggressive actions to return the bailout.

No wonder that the United States recovered the money lent to banks from the TARP with interests, while in Europe most of the bailouts have simply been lost money.

At the end of the day, markets have a healing effect, and the closer that regulation is to the reality of markets and supply and demand, the better.[4]

European politicians just do not understand that banks cannot reduce debt and expand credit everywhere at the same time.

Yet that is exactly what governments demand of the banking sector. More credit, but mass deleveraging.

Europe creates more than 200 pages of new regulation per week.[5]

This process of constant regulatory changes does not strengthen the financial sector balance sheets; it weakens them—because constant revisions sabotage the divestment and recapitalization process and introduce uncertainty, which scares demand, and valuations of the loan portfolios continue to erode, deepening the recession.

The European financial crisis was not a crisis of deregulation or of private banks—in 2006 fifty percent of European financial institutions were semistate-owned or controlled by politicians. There have been thousands of pages of regulations published every year since the creation of the EU

---

[4] A systemic approach to financial regulation A European perspective, Aglietta, Scialom, 2010.

[5] The rule of more, The Economist, 2012.

and the European Banking Association (EBA). Regulation and supervision in Europe is, and always has been, enormous.

This was a crisis of an economic model too dependent on commercial banks and a very intervened system.

Excessive, complex, and bureaucratic regulation has prolonged the agony of the industry for many years, instead of facilitating market conditions for the capital increases and asset sales needed.

Despite the detailed and complex regulation of the eurozone, between 2008 and 2011 Europe spent €4.5 trillion (37 percent of the GDP of the EU) in aid to financial institutions, many of them public and highly supervised.

More regulation will not solve the problem.

Europe's banks suffer what is called an "endogeneity problem."[6] Inward-looking. It is precisely excessive intervention that prevents a quick and surgical solution to financial sector difficulties.

As I said before, regulation must be effective and simple. In Europe, it is not. In the United States, it worsened.

The Eurogroup's resolution in 2013 about bank recapitalization—trying to avoid further bailouts with public funds—is an example of such endogenous problem. It was hailed as a success of the bail-in model,[7] but was far from it. First, because it did not close the door to unilateral state intervention, and second, because it did not facilitate the creation of prompt capitalization mechanisms in banks nor broke the mark-to-model perverse incentive.

The reader will not be surprised to know that, three years later, one of the main Italian banks had to be bailed out again with public funds.

By carrying out endless regulatory reviews, more than 26 in the past years, the Eurogroup creates uncertainty and banks cannot clean their balance sheets fast enough.

---

[6] Regulation of European Banks and Business Models, Centre for European Policy Studies, 2011.

[7] Covering bank losses with bondholders and shareholders' money, not public funds.

That cleanup cannot happen while governments borrow more, as banks in Europe accumulate up to 45 percent of countries' sovereign debt. Therefore, the "vicious circle" of financial-sovereign risk soars.

The prices of assets and loan portfolios deteriorate while the economic situation worsens by the constant tax increases and reductions in disposable income, creating a snowball effect.

Financial repression worsens the situation of the financial sector.

To prevent this deterioration, Europe introduces new volumes of hundreds of pages of regulation, again delaying any solution for the banks.

It has been more than eight years since European banks should have reduced debt aggressively. According to the ECB, by 2016 there has been only 35 percent deleveraging.

Banks need private capital and confidence to deleverage. The constant run-to-stand-still regulation overkill led to lower confidence and virtual impossibility to raise capital as shareholders fled the sector.[8]

In fact, emphasizing the risks to shareholders, bondholders, and depositors, but without solid recapitalization and liquidity mechanisms, is likely to generate even more public bailouts, because there might not be enough private money when needed, creating the perverse effect of accelerating what the agreement seeks to avoid. This is exactly what happened in Italy and Portugal in 2016.

There is not enough money between shareholders, bondholders, and the more than 100,000 euro deposits to cover the losses if a large bank experiences difficulties.

European countries each want to have their own financial sector "bound and controlled" but also with access to the purse of other eurozone members. This is what makes direct recapitalization such a moral hazard.

European banks have been an essential weapon for governments to artificially expand weak economies, placing the finance sector at risk without thinking of the consequences—a disturbing ignorance of what the core capital of a bank is and how quickly it fades out if economic and market conditions are not positive.

---

[8] Despite the ECB QE plan and calls for recovery, banks fell in the stock market between 50 and 60 percent in 2016.

The European financial sector is dangerously dependent on the strength of government debt. Few banks of the EU would survive a haircut on sovereign bonds, and the impact on businesses and citizens would be enormous. However, public debt continues to grow in almost all member countries because growth, consumption, and investment are torpedoed with financial repression.

Allowing growth and opening doors to investment and capital is the solution of all these communicating vessels that converge in the financial sector. Attracting capital and creating a favorable investment environment, with increased disposable income and economic growth, will recapitalize the banks—their assets would regain value, companies and families would be able to repay their debts, and the whole system would heal rapidly.

However, with financial repression and predatory regulation and intervention, politicians can agree on whatever they want in another committee, because the hole of the economy and state debt grows, and with them the difficulties for banks, in a downward spiral.

Banks had an undeniable responsibility in the crisis, but we cannot ignore governments' support of the excessive and artificial credit expansion of the period 2001 to 2011. They are two sides of the same coin. The solution to a decade of excess is not going to come in a few years.

Let's Stick Together

Central banks and governments form a unique alliance.

There is undeniable power in the fact that monetary policy is governed by independent members, but despite the constant reminders of the alleged central bank independence, the public and markets perceive an uncomfortable—and growing—link between central banks and governments.

Gone are the days when the governor of the central bank took uncomfortable decisions against the demands of reckless governments. The actions of BoJ are undeniably linked to the government and aimed at perpetuating imbalances until implosion.

The Federal Reserve has defended its independence numerous times, but questions were made in different times about surprising decisions.

If unemployment and inflation were the main targets, how come the Federal Reserve decided to postpone the decision to raise interest rates by a meager quarter of a percent until elections had passed in 2016?

When central bank decisions are less technical and the discourse changes, it creates a negative perception in citizens and too many perverse incentives in markets.

Central banks pay too much attention to financial assets and risks that they have created with excess confidence that there will be no consequences to artificial monetary expansion.

Governments forget structural reforms and supply-side measures and rely solely on monetary policy to disguise the imbalances until the next election, when the problem will be passed on to somebody else.

Governments need to realize that the long-term impact of forgetting supply-side measures and betting the entire house on low rates, devaluation, and spending means more taxes and less growth in the future.

As such, central banks need to add another layer to their policy.

Conditionality.

Governments cannot simply ask for more expansionary policies and sit back. Monetary policy must be conditioned to the implementation of fiscal reforms aimed at promoting stability, growth, and productivity.

Conditionality is not a penalty. It is about avoiding the accumulation of perverse incentives everywhere, starting—of course—with financial markets.

Central banks' conditionality to implementation of structural reforms is an essential tool to stop in its tracks any trading policy aimed at buying more when news is bad because monetary policy will be extended.

This factor of conditionality also helps the central banks avoid making mistakes that create further bubbles. It puts its own brakes.

The Taylor rule we mentioned in chapter 4 is part of that policy, but there are other relevant ways to adequately implement conditionality.

It has to be based on short-term and midterm policies, not just on vague calls for discipline. Governments will always prefer to spend more and be told off than to take the required actions and lose cheap money.

Implementing tax reforms to boost competitiveness, incentivizing investment in research and development, reducing unproductive subsidies to obsolete industries, and putting more money in families' pockets are essential drivers of an improvement of the growth model.

Denying overcapacity is a clear example. Europe, again, continues to go from stimulus plan to Juncker plan to Moscovici's infrastructure program and no one asks the question "what for?".

In any case, the reader will think that perverse incentives will not disappear, but the aim of this book is to provide an in-depth analysis and to realistically offer solutions to avoid the next big crash.

Conditionality, credit monitoring, mark-to-market, and limit on money supply to relative GDP growth are not "antigrowth" measures, but "pro–sustainable growth" ones.

Markets, governments, and central banks will always try to find excuses for imbalances. The important lesson here is that all can benefit from limiting the reckless behavior of one another, and everyone, particularly tax payers, will benefit from a process that limits boom and bust as the preferred policy method.

Central banks, governments, and markets have placed too large a bet on solving economies with policies that seem to give aggressive headlines but forget the most important factors: Families and Businesses.

The entire escape from the central bank trap depends on families and businesses recovering confidence, having more of their own money to save and spend, and investing wisely when required—not when mainstream economists and media tell them to—and on focusing policymakers' actions on balance, not bubbles.

CHAPTER 11

How to Get Out of Expansive Policies

"I'll break away, yes I'm on my way"

—Journey

There is nothing easier to do than to print money.

It feels great at first. Lord Keynes stated that, through monetary policy, they had found the way to turn stones into bread. There is plenty of wealth around, and the government can create all the money it needs to suits everyone's requirements. It simply does not work. And citizens and voters all over the world feel financial repression and are reacting against it—maybe not understanding its cause—more and more radically.

If there is one thing that strikes me as crazy about this time of uncontrolled debt, it is that mainstream media remains convinced that spending and stimulus policies are "social."

Many of these errors come from the glorification of Roosevelt's New Deal, although UCLA studies and others[1] prove that the intervention policy prolonged the Depression another seven years. And it is also a mistake to assume that solutions to modern crises should come from the same as the Great Depression, when our time is the result of that same expense and credit excess that today we are told is the solution. Recent crises are the result of endless "New Deals" stacked one against the other.

---

[1] FDR's Folly: How Roosevelt and His New Deal Prolonged the Great Depression, Burton W. Folsom, Jim Powell, Foundation of Economic Education, 2010.

The New Deal That Failed

The Great Depression dragged on for almost 15 years.

Analyzing President Roosevelt's record for four years, Harold L. Cole and Lee E. Ohanian concluded in a 2004 study[2] that New Deal policies signed into law thwarted economic recovery for seven long years due to anti-competition measures that Roosevelt promoted and signed into law on June 16, 1933.

> President Roosevelt believed that excessive competition was responsible for the Depression by reducing prices and wages and by extension reducing employment and demand for goods and services; so, he came up with a recovery package that would be unimaginable today: allowing businesses in every industry to collude without the threat of antitrust prosecution and workers to demand salaries about 25 percent above where they ought to have been, given market forces. The economy was poised for a beautiful recovery, but that recovery was stalled by these misguided policies.[3]

Meg Sullivan explained it in an article in UCLA.[4] In the three years following the implementation of Roosevelt's policies, wages in 11 key industries averaged 25 percent higher than they otherwise would have done, the economists calculate. But unemployment was also 25 percent higher than it should have been, given gains in productivity.

Meanwhile, prices across 19 industries averaged 23 percent above where they should have been, given the state of the economy. With goods and services that much harder for consumers to afford, demand stalled, and the gross national product floundered at 27 percent below where it otherwise might have been.

---

[2] New Deal Policies and the Persistence of the Great Depression: A General Equilibrium Analysis Harold L. Cole and Lee E. Ohanian, Journal of Political Economy, Vol. 112, No. 4 (August 2004).

[3] Harold L. Cole, professor of economics, UCLA.

[4] http://newsroom.ucla.edu/releases/FDR-s-Policies-Prolonged-Depression-5409

The policies were contained in the National Industrial Recovery Act (NIRA), which exempted industries from antitrust prosecution if they agreed to enter into collective bargaining agreements that significantly raised wages. Because protection from antitrust prosecution all but ensured higher prices for goods and services, a wide range of industries took the bait, Cole and Ohanian find. By 1934 more than 500 industries, which accounted for nearly 80 percent of private, nonagricultural employment, had entered into the collective bargaining agreements called for under NIRA.

Cole and Ohanian calculate that NIRA and its aftermath account for 60 percent of the weak recovery. Without the policies, they contend that the Depression would have ended in 1936 instead of the year when they believe the slump actually ended: 1943.

NIRA's role in prolonging the Depression has not been more closely scrutinized because the Supreme Court declared the act unconstitutional within two years of its passage.

Unemployment persisted. By 1939 the U.S. unemployment rate was 17.2 percent, down somewhat from its 1933 peak of 24.9 percent but still remarkably high. By comparison, in May 2003, the unemployment rate of 6.1 percent was the highest in 9 years.

Recovery came only after the Department of Justice dramatically stepped up enforcement of antitrust cases nearly fourfold and organized labor suffered a string of setbacks, the economists find.

"The fact that the Depression dragged on for years convinced generations of economists and policy makers that capitalism could not be trusted to recover from depressions and that significant government intervention was required to achieve good outcomes," Cole said. "Ironically, our work shows that the recovery would have been very rapid had the government not intervened."[5]

Some criticize this analysis. Eric Rauchway[6] states:

---

[5] From an article and interview by Meg Sullivan, FDR's policies prolonged Depression by 7 years, UCLA economists calculate, 2004.

[6] FDR's Latest Critics, Was the New Deal un-American? Eric Rauchway 2007.

If the New Deal did not end the Great Depression, was it doing some good? Historical Statistics of the United States says yes: Except in the 1937–38 recession, unemployment fell every year of the New Deal. Also, real GDP grew at an annual rate of around 9 percent during Roosevelt's first term and, after the 1937–38 dip, around 11 percent.

However, in the 1930s unemployment never fell below 15 percent. Five years into the New Deal, one in five U.S. citizens in the labor force were unemployed. In 1937 there were six million unemployed. By 1938 the figure rose to 10 million.

Unfortunately, it was not Roosevelt but the war that reduced unemployment. Around 20 percent of the workforce was absorbed by the war industry, with 42 percent of GDP spent in the process. However, inflation during the period was very high (close to 20 percent), and even with 1 percent unemployment there was rationing of basic products.

The United States finally escaped the Depression when the war ended; it cut 33 percent of taxes and started to lift barriers to competition.

The reality of hundreds of cases since then is that massive government intervention trying to fix the economy and putting limits to trade and competition creates a larger imbalance, slower recoveries, and—rapidly— another crisis.

At least defenders of Roosevelt's policies should be intellectually honest to understand that undertaking government-spending stimuli when debt and spending are low and there is no slack in the economy is not the same as when debt stands at 100 percent of GDP, deficits are already huge, government spending exceeds 30 percent of GDP, and overcapacity remains.

Roosevelt multiplied debt by more than 10, from $22.5 billion to $258.5 billion, from 34 to 95 percent of GDP … but this included a world war! Today we are under the illusion that debt amounting to 100 percent of GDP is OK even in times of peace.

Even considering a world war, government spending under Roosevelt never rose above 25 percent…. Before the horrible event of such a war, spending never rose above … 12.5 percent!

And we call for New Deals today at an average government spend of 30 to 50 percent of GDP in the main OECD economies?

The dangerous thing is that we have seen nothing but "new deals" for decades. We live in a perennial New Deal with diminishing returns.

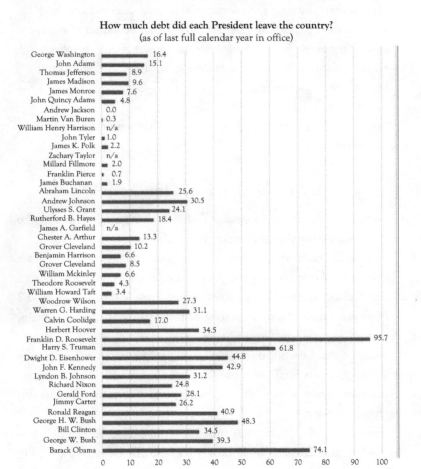

How much debt did each President leave the country?
(as of last full calendar year in office)

Public debt as a share of GDP (percent)

Source: Congressional Budget Office.

Yet defenders of inflationism and endless money creation resort time and time again to the messages we mentioned before: "It could have been worse," and "This time it's different." Repeat.

Sorry, citizens all over the world do not accept this anymore.

Ludwig von Mises explained:

There is no use in arguing with people who are driven by "an almost religious fervour" and believe that their master "had the Revelation." It is one of the tasks of economics to analyse carefully each of the inflationist plans, those of Keynes and Gesell no less than those of their innumerable predecessors from John Law down to Major Douglas. Yet, no one should expect that any logical argument or any experience could ever shake the almost religious fervour of those who believe in salvation through spending and credit expansion.[7]

In fact, citizens perceive that something is happening. In their pockets; in their wealth.

We Are Turning Bread Into Stones

And economic agents, policy makers, and investors must do something to avoid this increasing tide of completely justified rage.

The rise of protectionism, resistance to globalization, and the embrace of populism and extreme views surprise many. How can this happen when the EU, United States, and Japan's policies are made for "their own good"?

How can citizens be so ungrateful to turn against the EU in Britain, or against Obama in the United States, and so on ...?

Many of them do not understand that a very relevant reason for the rise of inequality is financial repression and QEs, which disproportionately benefit those who have access to widespread credit and whose wealth is in financial assets.[8]

Standard and Poor's, in 2016, noted that the Bank of England's monetary policy measures alleviated the impact of the financial crisis of 2008 to 2009 and aided an economic recovery, but their side effects amplified wealth disparities, mainly by boosting financial asset prices and house prices.

---

[7] Stones into Bread: The Keynesian Miracle, Ludwig von Mises. Plain Talk, March 1948.

[8] QE And Economic Inequality. Standard & Poor's, 10-Feb-2016.

The share of net financial wealth held by the wealthiest 10 percent of the population rose notably in the aftermath of the financial crisis, from 56 percent in 2008 to 65 percent in 2014, suggesting that wealthier households were able to anticipate and take advantage of financial market developments since the onset of QE, increasing their wealth in absolute and relative terms.

The reason for this disconnect between the size of QE and economic performance is partially the transmission channel from QE to the economy.

When the central bank buys government bonds, the sellers of those government bonds should move out the risk spectrum and buy more risky assets, including credit and private equity.

This does not happen, or at least to the extent that policymakers would want it to happen. Money goes to liquid financial assets. See Figure 11.1.

As such, investors pile up on more of the assets that are "guaranteed" by central bank buying. But it is also a mistake in the diagnosis.

Central banks believe it is a problem of incentivizing demand and credit, and it is not. So, excess liquidity does not change the behavior of economic agents. It makes the financial experts richer.

The easy response to the rise of income inequality is to blame capitalism—when it has nothing to do with capitalism—and, even worse, demand redistribution at all costs.

Figure 11.1 Stock market becomes more expensive

Source: Bloomberg.

As we have noted before, these are ineffective measures. More government control, "creation of money for the people," and higher taxation are no solutions to abnormalities caused by government intervention, money printing, and excess taxation.[9]

Redistribution policies have a positive effect when supply-side measures and growth of the private sector and wealth are not penalized. When redistribution is the only policy, it just obliterates prosperity.

In fact, voters are not voting against inequality. Few are against fair inequality when success is granted and hard work justifies it. Very few complain about the salary of successful artists and top entrepreneurs, great athletes, or job creators. That is why the votes that have surprised the most—Brexit, Trump, and so on—were not in favor of socialist inflationist measures, but in favor of old-school trickle-down.

No one has ever died of inequality; it is poverty that kills. And beggar-thy-neighbor is not a social policy. It is impoverishment by decree.

The reader might disagree and call monetary expansion a failure of capitalism, but it has nothing to do with capitalism and a lot to do with socialist views of providing unique and excessive incentives to governments and crony sectors so that they can access capital against the savings and wealth of SMEs and families.

Even if the reader disagrees, the question is simple. How do we get out of expansionary policies without another financial crisis that hurts, again, households and taxpayers the most?

Expansionary policies cannot last forever, and—as we saw with QE3—even defenders are more than surprised at how rapidly their idea of wealth effect and stability disappears.

Banks Don't Benefit

There is nothing easier than entering a period of money-supply expansion. It is a central banker's dream. It promises great success and easy solutions to complex problems, the governor becomes famous, spends

---

[9] The Paradox of Redistribution and Strategies of Equality: Welfare State Institutions, Inequality, and Poverty in the Western Countries. Walter Korpi and Joakim Palme. February 1998.

hours on end in TV and radio interviews and everybody assumes he or she is the savior, Merlin the magician with a magic wand.

Some mention that banks are the main beneficiaries of QE. Not really. Negative rates and excess liquidity have had little discernible positive impact on banks. Margins collapse; lending is more difficult; and the positive impact on lower borrowing cost is more than offset by weaker margins.

The "positive effect" of the ECB offering a negative interest on liquidity does not reach 17 basis points in Net Income Margin (NIM). However, the negative effect of the erosion of margins in the European banks' loans and deposits due to artificially low rates exceeded 89 basis points during 2015 to 2016, according to Mediobanca,[10] which resulted in an average drop of up to 20 percent in their profits, with an increase default risk.

In Europe's case, it could not be clearer. Since the ECB QE was launched until end of 2016, earnings of banks have fallen in absolute terms, relative to expectations, and the index also fell more than 25 percent. The Euro Stoxx Financials is down more than 50 percent since 2009.

The problem is getting out when so many—and such massively large—sectors are hanging by the thread of excess liquidity.

Mainstream View

Once in a liquidity trap, mainstream considers two means of escape.

The first is to use expansionary fiscal policy. The problem, in heavily indebted economies with relevant pockets of industrial overcapacity, is that expansionary fiscal policies tend to be "governments spending more," and we have seen in previous chapters that infrastructure spending and traditional demand-side policies increased deficits and white elephants, create no further growth and leave the debt and the operating costs of the infrastructure project. Economies become less dynamic and taxes rise afterwards, to pay for the bill.

The second means is to lower the zero nominal interest rate floor. This option involves paying negative interest on government "bearer

[10] Keep Surfin the QE Tidal Wave, Antonio Guglielmi, Mediobanca, 2015.

bonds"—coin and currency, that is "taxing money," as advocated by Gesell. This would also reduce the likelihood of ending up in a liquidity trap.

Again, it does not happen. Negative rates make banks and economic agents be more cautious, and investors prefer to receive a small negative return than to lose more money in other asset classes. Money goes to Gold Exchange Traded Funds (ETFs), short-term speculative liquid assets.

Taxing currency amounts to having periodic "currency reforms," that is, compulsory conversions of "old" currency into "new" currency, say, by stamping currency. The terms of the conversion can be set to achieve any positive or negative interest rate on currency. There are likely to be significant shoe-leather costs associated with such schemes. The policy question then becomes: How much shoe leather does it take to fill an output gap?[11] The answer is evident. The output gap might not widen but is perpetuated through real negative rates. In the previous chapters, we have seen how futile it is to try to encourage demand through financial repression.

In 2003, Svensson even talked of the "foolproof way"[12] to exit a liquidity trap. The "optimal" way involved three elements: (1) an explicit central-bank commitment to a higher future price level; (2) a concrete action that demonstrates the central bank's commitment, induces expectations of a higher future price level, and jump-starts the economy; and (3) an exit strategy that specifies when and how to get back to normal.

Of course, this so-called foolproof way, which is exactly what mainstream recommended and central banks implemented point by point, resulted in lower growth, more debt, and financial asset bubbles. By 2016 even mainstream economists were talking of secular stagnation. The problem with these solutions is that all of them ignored structural reforms and the importance of paying attention to the impact of ever-expanding financial repression on the disposable income of consumers. The concerns of businesses about the economy were also ignored.

---

[11] Further read: Liquidity Traps: How to Avoid Them and How to Escape Them. Willem H. Buiter, Nikolaos Panigirtzoglou. NBER Working Paper No. 7245, July 1999.
[12] Escaping from a Liquidity Trap and Deflation: The Foolproof Way and Others. Lars E.O. Svensson, NBER Working Paper No. 10195, December 2003.

Believing in central planning to work its magic to deliver growth is rarely under question in most mainstream papers. If it fails, it is not because of central-planned alchemy, but because the recipe to convert stones into bread has a missing ingredient.

This approach can be found in Werning,[13] who states that monetary policy promotes both inflation and an output boom, even if the latter is more than doubted. He proposes a decomposition of spending according to "opportunistic" and "stimulus" motives. This approach has also been tried over and over, but it always fails when the key variables, debt saturation and slack in the economy, remain, because both spending items add and perpetuate the imbalances that slow down the economy.

Others are more balanced. Schmitt-Grohé and Uribe's interest-rate-based Taylor rule option[14] looks at a policy designed to raise inflationary expectations over time while at the same time maintaining the Taylor principle close to the intended inflation target. What this theory looks for is a short-term "boost" from interest rates that does not require an accompanying fiscalist (or non-Ricardian) fiscal stance. This "balanced expansion" approach makes sense when the excess savings of families and businesses come from too high a cost of borrowing, and these economic agents would be willing to spend more and invest if financial conditions were looser. None of those cases happened in the formation of the OECD central bank trap. Interest rates were already extremely low and access to credit was plentiful—for credible projects with a real economic return. This approach was followed by the ECB, among others.

Supply-Side Is the Answer

My opinion differs entirely from these—already failed—options. Because the best way to exit a liquidity trap is not to create a bigger one. But what to do once it has happened?

---

[13] Managing a Liquidity Trap: Monetary and Fiscal Policy. Iván Werning, MIT, 2010.

[14] Liquidity Traps: An Interest-Rate-Based Exit Strategy, Stephanie Schmitt-Grohé, Martín Uribe. NBER Working Paper No. 16514, Issued in November 2010.

The first thing we should note is that, yes, markets will fall and yields will rise. It is ridiculous to think it will not happen after inflating asset prices for years.

What's important is to help citizens and SMEs separate the idea that financial markets are a reflection of the real economy and that something that, as we noted before, they have little exposure to, will not cause them harm.

This reduction in irrational exuberance can happen gradually while investors find more attractive opportunities in the real economy.

How can this happen?

Tax cuts are an essential factor. Letting the economy breathe, helping SMEs thrive, letting consumption rise, and allowing savings—yes, savings—to improve.

Wealth and prosperity always come from saving, not from debt.

The idea that it is better for governments to spend the money that others do not want to spend and therefore not cut taxes because citizens could—evil beings those—decide to save part of it is pure nonsense. First, because it is their hard-earned money and, second, because there is no evidence that the government knows better what has to be done with money.

Every time I read estimates of future tax revenues if countries raised taxes to "the rich" and large companies, I am amazed at the naivety of thinking that everyone affected is going to stay put and not react. I've never seen a single estimate reflect the potential loss of economic activity.

All these "expected revenues" assume that nothing would change. And I am dismayed at how little we look abroad.

And tax disincentives lead to Inversion Deals.

What are they?

Imagine that a company gets charged very high taxes. It may decide to acquire or merge with another in a tax-friendly country and move the corporate headquarters to that nation. Thus, the new group, with all the strategic reasons to merge, benefits from a preferential tax treatment.

The merged company must have less than 80 percent of its shareholder base in the United States, and at least 25 percent of the activity of the new group should be generated in the new headquarter center.

The problem, in most of the cases, is not only the tax burden, but the bureaucracy and the obstacles to generating economic activity. Many of the companies that left the United States for Canada or Ireland did it also because the conditions for their activity were more attractive.

Given the complexity of making the change to a different country, these transactions generally have a very clear strategic logic. Mergers "criticized" by the U.S. government since 2004 have created more than six million jobs worldwide and globally generate higher tax revenues in the countries where they operate.[15]

According to Congress, between 2015 and 2024, $18.5 billion of tax revenue could be lost to inversion. There was, however, no talk about how much more the United States could earn by lowering the corporate tax rate by five points, if we assume the same margins and profits of 2014 and an annual 1.6 percent growth in GDP.[16]

That concern for "lost revenue" would not exist if taxes went down. Is it a race to zero where the other countries would lower their tax rate even more? Of course not, as companies work with many scales of risk and opportunity. If taxation is competitive, it will not move because of small differences. There are many relevant factors.

Corporate tax rate in the United States is one of the highest in the OECD. Rather than reducing it, laws were implemented to avoid inversion deals, one in 1983 and another in 2004. Congress imposed its "American Jobs Creation Act" of 2004. Of course, before long, inversion deals accelerated. Between 2007 and 2014 more companies left the United States to more business-friendly countries than in the entire period from 1981 to 2003, according to the Congressional Research Service.

Legislative repression and calls to patriotism, even inflammatory proclamations to "boycott" companies, have failed. The new administration in 2017 was looking at lowering the corporate tax to 17 percent, which is a logical step.

Tax receipts grow with economic activity, not because of a committee decision.

Does this mean no taxes and no public services? No. It means more efficient use of the vast resources that governments have, with the majority

---

[15] According to UBS. "A New Wave of Tax Inversions, 2015."

[16] Not a counterfactual. The impact of lower taxes on economic output has been discussed with empiric papers in chapter 10.

of it used for the best investment the public sector can undertake, and more support for education and health care. Note the word "support." Let us not confuse education and health care with using the subterfuge to increase imbalances and wasteful spending, even less so confusing education with indoctrination.

Tax cuts are essential to let the economy recover and help disposable income rise when the uncertainty about the economy and labor market might not increase wages.[17]

As the economy recovers investment, consumption, and growth, wages will rise as overcapacity is reduced or eliminated and slack disappears from the economy.

Raising interest rates is essential to reduce overcapacity and allow banks to recover.

The current disproportionately low interest rate perpetuates overcapacity, and velocity of money and productivity fall.

This will allow some creative destruction in obsolete sectors, banks will be able to lend at rates that are closer to the real risk, and the engine of growth will come from higher-productivity sectors that do not need hidden subsidies of devaluation and low rates to thrive.

Structural reforms have to happen in the form of lower spending with higher efficiency, but also clear reforms that support investment in research and development at the private-sector level, so that investigation has a clear economic return and companies have strong chances to grow and thereby demand more jobs.

Promoting entrepreneurial behavior and the creation of new companies is also essential to tackle the slack in the labor market. Focus on creating your own job rather than finding it.

Central banks must at the same time have a very clear timeframe of monetary policy unwinding that does not fall under the cliff, killing credibility.

The Federal Reserve cannot promise four rate hikes and deliver one, when nonfarm payroll data remains solid and growth remains. Maybe the slowdown can justify only two rate hikes but not one. Credibility is

[17] What Is the Evidence on Taxes and Growth? William McBride, 2010. Tax Foundation.

essential so that financial markets do not take the warnings and communication as irrelevant because "it will not happen."

Unwinding monetary policy has to happen with the previously mentioned target of confirming that structural reforms are implemented and government spending is controlled. Conditionality, as such, is key.

Beware of financial markets. Animal spirits cannot dictate a policy that is aimed at restoring disposable income, wealth, and opportunities for nonfinancial jobs and families.

But they cannot be ignored. Therefore, a concerted communication policy from government to media to central banks to avoid excess risk-taking must be accompanied by bold microeconomic measures of tax incentives, growth policies, and evidence that the private sector is back, hiring and investing with confidence.

Government deficit spending is an integral part of that confidence build. Deficits mean higher taxes in the future, or large imbalances that will surface through a crisis or high unemployment, when the placebo effect ends.

Therefore, control of deficits is an integral part of confidence-building. The EU has made an effort in this matter. But not enough.

The financial sector should continue to be monitored and use a period of higher rates to continue to build core capital and write down nonperforming loans. It will be a difficult period, but not any more challenging than the 2014 to 2016 period, and the entities will become stronger, with higher access to private capital while margins improve.

But the financial sector cannot be just a bet on banks improving. Economies with a large problem of overcapacity and excessive dependency on bank finance of the real economy must undertake structural reforms as well to help diversify and modernize the financing of SMEs and families, through fintech and crowdfunding or crowdlending.

All these are measures that need to be implemented with clear and immediate objectives to avoid the mistake of Japan, which "forgot" the third arrow.

In summary, these policies that we have outlined in this part come from the necessary recovery of credibility while citizens perceive a strong commitment to end the perverse incentives of what has been called the establishment, maybe unfairly. But it is important to have adequate checks and balances, with not just incentives, but disincentives when the correct measures are not taken.

We have lived more than 50 years in a world in which the dominant factors in economic and monetary policy have been demand-side measures and wrongly named "expansionary" measures, which has led to massive boom and bust cycles that happen more frequently and leave more of the middle class behind.

It is time to go back to supply-side policies, where moderate inflation is not an objective, but the result of improved growth that puts disposable income at the forefront. It is also time to end the dominance of financial markets as something to "pamper" through ever-rising asset prices; financial markets should provide capital and liquidity to the real economy so it can thrive in high-productivity areas, not cheap money for low-productivity white elephants.

Supply-side policies aim to enable the free market to work more efficiently by reducing government interference and by improving the economy looking at the benefits of higher competition, free markets, and improved productivity.

Reducing bureaucracy and barriers to entry to boost competitiveness.

Limiting government action in the economy to the role of simple and effective regulation, moving away from direct intervention in specific economic sectors, reducing unproductive subsidies, cutting red tape, and allowing competition to absorb overcapacity and improve technology and development.

Cutting income taxes and corporate taxes to boost growth, increasing consumption, and allowing deleverage to happen while economic growth is in place.

More private research and development, education, and training aimed at maximizing the output and real economic return of investments in research and development, with the focus on ideas that become startups, and in turn, companies, boosting jobs and growth. Education and training to adapt to a world that is rapidly changing and where students and citizens need to learn to become "leaders in change."

Reducing government spending without compromising service and quality. Health care and education cannot be measured by how much is spent, but by how successful they are at delivering the service and quality required. Efficiency programs to focus public spend on real service, not increased budget management.

Slashing unnecessary red tape and bureaucracy which add to a business's cost without any productive improvement to the economy.

Develop modern infrastructure without perverse incentives. A private-sector infrastructure program financed by tolls and tax incentives, not direct subsidies.

Supply-side policies play a role in fighting a low aggregate demand that traps an economy at the "zero lower bound" (ZLB) of nominal interest rates. Future increases in productivity or reductions in costs triggered by supply-side policies generate a stronger wealth effect than demand-side or QE measures do. This, in turn, pulls up current consumption and output. Since the economy is already at zero and negative interest rates, small increases do not undo this wealth effect.[18]

Demand-side policies had logic when government spending was less than 20 percent of GDP and there was an immediate and evident need for industrial and productive capacity, but the evidence of the past two decades is of saturation of such policies and too much debt.

There is a tremendous potential for developed economies if we forget the paradigm of growth via debt and recover the objective to rebuild the middle class by placing disposable income and saving at the forefront of policy.

This is the only way the world will escape the central bank trap without creating another financial crisis.

---

[18] Supply-Side Policies and the Zero Lower Bound, Jesús Fernández-Villaverde, Pablo A. Guerrón-Quintana, Juan Rubio-Ramírez, NBER Working Paper No. 17543, October 2011.

CHAPTER 12

The Investors' Guide to Secular Stagnation

"I've been around, seen some things, I slept in dumpsters, got high with kings"

—Kid Rock

I have had numerous meetings with investors where the main message is something like this:

The investor feels stocks and bonds are very expensive, that private equity is too risky, and that low rates and devaluation put at risk their savings. What can they do?

The first—and most important—step is to really understand your profile as an investor.

How Risk Averse I Am

One of the things that financial repression has done to the average investor is to completely obliterate tolerance for volatility.

I remember once being called to appear on TV to talk about the "stock market crash." I asked myself what the hell had happened because I didn't notice. It turned out that the market had fallen 2 percent. Two percent. "A crash."

Media and mainstream consensus fell so comfortably under the central bank trap that perception of risk disappeared and, with it, the idea that stocks and bonds do become too expensive and the marginal buyer loses confidence.

Look in the mirror and ask yourself which type of investor you really are.

I heard once from a client: "I am very conservative; I am OK with 5 to 6 percent." This in an era where the lowest risk assets were yielding negative returns. Obviously, he did not analyze risk appetite adequately.

The central bank trap can be a good source of returns, but we also must understand that, by 2016, there are two consecutive generations of traders that have seen nothing but expansionary policies.

Therefore, we must understand our risk appetite and at the same time find good managers that are able to discern value and opportunities without repeating that "long term everything goes up."

Bonds

When we hear, correctly, that there is a large bubble in bonds, might be too simplistic.

Not all bonds are the same.

Let us understand first why we see the bubble in bonds. Low-risk sovereign bonds yield negative or virtually zero returns and inflation expectations are rising. Therefore, bondholders that have some of these assets in their portfolio are likely to see three things:

- Negative nominal and real returns, that is, losses, on the portfolio
- Outflows of capital from ultralow yield bonds, which make them even less liquid
- A global perception that there is more value in equities, creating higher volatility

So, the first thing that the central bank trap shows us is the disproportionate risk-reward ratio in the allegedly safest assets. They become very expensive and very illiquid quickly.

The second area of risk is in High Yield. Many investors might perceive that, when inflation rises and the U.S. 10-year bond sees a better yield, it does not make sense to buy bonds of companies with very high risk and challenged fundamentals because the risk-reward is, again, disproportionate.

But there are plenty of other options.

As the Escape from the Central Bank Trap should dictate, investors must seek to cover their portfolio from the risk of stagflation and recession at the same time … and inflation-linked bonds from Investment Grade[1] companies and sovereigns.

Inflation-linked bonds (ILBs) are designed to help protect investors from the negative impact of inflation by contractually linking the bonds' principal and interest payments to a nationally recognized inflation measure such as the Retail Price Index (RPI) in the UK, the European Harmonized Index of Consumer Prices (HICP) ex-tobacco in Europe, and the Consumer Price Index (CPI) in the United States.[2]

Together with inflation accrual and coupon payments, the third driver of ILBs' total return comes from the price fluctuation due to changes in real yields. If the bond is held to maturity, the price change component becomes irrelevant; however, prior to expiration, the market value of the bond moves higher or lower than its par amount.

Just like nominal bonds, whose prices move in response to nominal interest-rate changes, ILB prices will increase as real yields decline and decrease as real yields rise. Should an economy undergo a period of deflation—a sustained decline in price levels during the life of an ILB, the inflation-adjusted principal could decline below its par value. Subsequently, coupon payments would be based on this deflation-adjusted amount. See Figure 12.1. However, many ILB-issuing countries, such as the United States, Australia, France, and Germany, offer deflation floors at maturity: if deflation drives the principal amount below par, an investor would still receive the full par amount at maturity. So, while coupon payments are paid on a principal adjusted for inflation or deflation, an investor receives the greater of the inflation-adjusted principal or the initial par amount at maturity.

This instrument is flexible enough to provide the type of security that some investors demand and a certain kicker if inflation grows. But they are not zero-risk instruments, the investor must assess the ability of the issuer to pay the maturities and coupon, as well as the risk of suffering in

---

[1] Those companies whose credit fundamentals are highest rated.
[2] Source: PIMCO education.

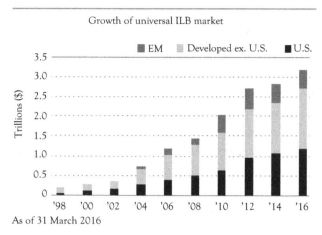

Figure 12.1 Inflation-linked bonds have become very popular

Source: Barclays; PIMCO.

the price of the bond if inflation happens and the issuing country or the currency of the issuer is significantly devalued.

Bonds are not a zero-risk asset; there is no such thing as an asset with no risk.

Other popular bonds in this environment as we escape the central bank trap are those of emerging market companies whose revenues are in dollars because they are well diversified and their debt is in local currency or fully linked to the currency of their revenues. Especially if these companies have costs in local currency, these instruments have proven to be a good hedge against aggressive devaluations, sudden stop, and fluctuations in commodities.

Equities

Equities have been a tricky asset in the period of financial repression. Returns vary between sectors and the overall good performance of indexes has also been clouded by a diminishing inflow of capital.

Calls for a "great rotation" from bonds into equities did not happen in the years of the central bank trap because the entire focus of governments, central bankers, and companies was on the fixed-income market. This made investors prefer an asset class that everyone is adamant to protect over equities, where volatility and yield appeared attractive but not enough to make the switch. The prospects of profit warnings, capital increases, and weak returns in a secular stagnation did just that.

However, as we escape the central bank trap, we see that the global earnings recession that we entered in 2008 could be close to an end thanks to a pickup in inflation and improved fundamentals in countries that look to boost growth through tax cuts and supply-side measures, such as the United States.

Escaping the central bank trap involves enormous volatility, and the investor must acknowledge this risk. This is no time to talk macro and make grand statements about stocks in general.

The investor will have to focus on picking stocks where fundamentals remain attractive despite the asset inflation of the past years.

In order to do that, investors will have to analyze trends and multiples. For me, the most important combination is that of strong Free Cash Flow Yield, a Return on Capital Employed that stands a few points higher than Weighted Average Cost of Capital (WACC) (as we explained in previous chapters), and a strong balance sheet. What is most important is that the company's management interests are aligned with those of minority investors, by having a sizeable part of their remuneration in shares and solid targets that can be monitored on a quarterly basis as the company publishes earnings.

Diversification is key, but so is recognizing the strength of the equities portfolio that investors create. Such strength will only happen if we have one sentence in mind:

Cycles are becoming shorter and more abrupt, and portfolios should be protected by being active at selling once decent returns have been achieved and churning the portfolio to adapt to new opportunities that come from the change of cycle. See Table 12.1.

Keith McCullough explains how cycles matter:

> The run-up is supported by cold-hard economic data. U.S. growth and inflation are finally accelerating and the investing implications are actually quite simple. You sell bonds. You buy stocks.
>
> Here's why.
>
> Unlike casual macro "tourists," I'm not wedded to opinions or how something "feels." The only thing that truly matters is the

Table 12.1 Sectors that perform in economic cycles

Economic cycle stage	Characteristics	Business cycle industries that do well in this stage	Examples
Expansion: Early Stage	Low, increasing inflation Low, increasing interest rates High unused capacity Low inventory	*Cyclicals* **Consumer credit:** Firms that are tied to the housing industry **Energy:** Companies that produce energy-related products **Consumer cyclicals:** Manufactures of consumer products that respond to the changes in disposable income	Savings and loans, regional banks Oil, coal Advertising, apparel, auto manufacturers, retailers
Expansion: Middle Stage	Moderate inflation Moderate interest rates Moderate unused capacity Moderate inventory	**Basic materials:** Companies manufacturing materials (not machinery) to produce finished goods **Technology:** Companies manufacturing high-tech products for consumers and businesses	Chemicals, plastics, paper, wood, metals Semiconductors, computer hardware, software and services, communications equipment
Expansion: Late State	High inflation High interest rates Low unused capacity High inventory	**Capital goods:** Companies manufacturing machinery used to produce finished goods **Financials:** Firms tied to loans that are in demand due to economic expansion **Transportation:** Companies that transport goods and passengers	Equipment and machinery manufactures Corporate and institutional bankers Airlines, trucking railroad
Recession	Decreasing inflation Decreasing interest rates Increasing unused capacity Decreasing inventory	*Defensive* **Consumer staples:** Manufactures of basic consumer products that are purchased at largely the same level through all economic cycles **Utilities:** Regulated companies providing products and services such as electricity	Food, drugs, cosmetics, tobacco, liquor Electric gas, water
Independent of Economic Cycles	Varied economic circumstances	*Growth* *Industries and companies in the early stage of a life cycle:* Expanding quickly and not subject to economic cycles	Biotechnology

Source: Wayne Thorp.

data. On that front, U.S. economic data has been decidedly bull-ish for two straight months:

Industrial Production: U.S. Industrial Production registered its first positive reading in 15 months this week, or +0.5 percent year-over-year growth. That snapped the longest streak of negative growth ever outside of protracted U.S. recessions.

Consumer Price Index: Headline Inflation accelerated for a 5th consecutive month, taking consumer price growth to its highest level in 32 months (since May 2014) at +2.1 percent in December. This effectively ended 30 straight months of inflation readings that were stubbornly below the Fed's 2 percent target.

Add this to the long list of economic indicators now realizing positive year-over-year growth:

- Wage Growth
- ISM (Institute for Supply Management) Manufacturing
- Durable Goods (ex-Defense and Aircraft)
- Auto Sales
- Retail Sales
- Disposable Personal Income Growth[3]

These are extremely important factors to understand opportunities. Growth accelerating versus growth slowing. It might surprise some that these trends change in six months, but that is because we are sold by cen-tral planners to believe that cycles are five years long or more. They are not.

That is why it is so important to follow the advice of real-time inves-tors that have no agenda to prove and who simply follow the hard data, providing recommendations that include indicators of cycle turns, over-sold and overbought, and differentiated views from consensus.

Consensus leads only to mediocrity, as I stated in my book *Life In The Financial Markets,* and it is very important to understand the macro and micro elements of investing while at the same time following a unique approach.

---

[3] Buy Stocks, Sell Bonds! The Economy Is Accelerating.

Stocks are complicated, but only if you follow the same approach as everyone else and trust investment bank recommendations. However, once one understands that the macro elements do not have to be awesome or terrible, just accelerating or decelerating, and that real multiples of cash flow and returns growth matter, the challenges of equity investment are greatly reduced.

The Escape from Central Bank Trap trade follows the simple, and at the same time complex, rule of analyzing the short-term trends and how they affect earnings to pick stocks that will give us a winning portfolio by recognizing cycles.

Some of the trends that seem to be clearer in this race to win against the central bank trap are:

Rise in Inflation comes mainly from commodities, so cycle must be analyzed to see whether the supply-demand picture of those commodities is delivered or becomes another trap.

Most economists are expecting a big increase in inflation. While there is obviously an important base effect from 2016 levels due to the stabilization of commodities, the underlying factors that drive inflation expectations remain weak. Not only is China's growth likely to disappoint, and with it its imports and purchasing power, but the compounded effect of technology, aging population in the OECD, and overcapacity count as stronger forces against inflation expectations than the rise in oil and food prices.

The biggest risk to this prediction is that the rise of protectionism affects world trade in a more severe way than expected and price rises due to lower trade are added to weak growth to cause stagflation. Core inflation, which is what matters to the economy, is likely to remain subdued, whatever happens with commodities. Oil is likely to lose momentum as supply cuts are proven ineffective, demand—especially from China—disappoints, and U.S. and Canada supplies surge.

The EU could emerge stronger from Brexit and local elections.

It is tempting to think that the EU will collapse and the euro will break up because of political turmoil. However, with each new local crisis, the underlying factors that strengthen the euro as a currency, technical and practical, overtake the evident threatening elements. This does not mean that Europe is going to grow above estimates to 2020, but the elections and banking crises continue to make the euro project more resistant, whether we like it or not.

China will not collapse, but will likely continue weakening further. China's imbalances were not reduced in 2016. The accumulation of debt and the massive real estate bubble, added to capital outflows, show that China is unable to tackle overcapacity and strengthen its growth model. However, growth of middle class, young population, and the fact that most imbalances are well known and denominated in local currency prevent a 2008-type collapse.

Emerging markets are likely to face sudden stop adequately and avoid collapse from strong dollar and capital outflows. Foreign exchange reserves in emerging markets have remained strong and recession and capital outflows have been tackled in the right way by most central banks. Although they are likely to face tough years, emerging economies are better prepared in 2017 for a difficult environment.

Gold and Bitcoin

A Nigerian citizen tweeted a very interesting case in 2016. He feared that his country's central bank would break parity with the U.S. dollar. Worried about losing all his savings and faced with a huge devaluation, he decided to move his deposits to a platform that makes transactions in gold backed 100 percent by physical gold. The currency fell almost 50 percent against the dollar overnight. His small savings appreciated.

This case is paradigmatic of a trend that is happening all over the world among citizens who are looking for an alternative that protects them from financial repression, allowing them to store value, and at the same time is compatible with traditional means of payment.

Those who have accumulated a portion of their savings, even their wages, in platforms fully backed by physical gold have not only seen their money grow, but platforms allow making transactions in different currencies without suffering fluctuations and volatility.

At the same time, the central banks of emerging markets have increased their reserves of dollars and gold.

Gold multiplied in value in the period into financial repression driven by the fear of many that the economies would suffer hyperinflation. Many investors were wrong because, as we explained, QE is disinflationary as it perpetuates debt and overcapacity while money velocity falls.

This "mistake" made gold lose its speculative appeal and gold-linked financial positions (ETFs) fell from almost 3,000 metric tons to less than 1,500, according to Goldman Sachs.

However, the risk of financial repression did not end, and many investors, from China to India, saw the risk of large devaluations and the demonetization of currencies, which could put their savings at risk. Risk perception of a global currency war increased.

Fear of the confiscation of savings through monetary policy also sky-rocketed, particularly in China, as capital flights increased.

And that is why those looking for a store of value, an inflation hedge and a risk hedge, a certain element of security in the face of an uncertain environment—or a very true fear—find gold attractive.

Despite the increasing Chinese, Russian, and Asian demand, Gold has been oversupplied since 2009 and reached its peak (almost 20 million ounces of overcapacity) in 2010. That trend has reversed over the past two years, and by 2016, supply is tight.

The problem for the Escape from the Central Bank Trap trade was that, for many, the purchase of gold as a reserve of value or investment was mainly via financial derivatives that are as risky as other financial products in a crisis, and are not backed by the physical precious metal. The difference with physical gold platforms that are growing all over the world is that they democratize the access to the physical trade by selling small parts of a bar of gold, but always clearly stating that it is 100 percent backed by such ingot.

Even those who, like me, think that the risk of a crisis like 2008 is mod-erately contained and that what we are facing is more a period of low growth and poor inflation due to saturation of stimuli, the continuous policy of attacking the saver and devaluing supports holding a portion of savings in gold.

It is not surprising that families and companies seek to mitigate the impact of financial repression via gold with guaranteed physical platforms.

Bitcoin is a completely different proposition. A digital currency that cannot be manipulated by central banks. The digital currency, whose sup-ply cannot be increased by political decisions, has seen record inflows from Chinese and Indian citizens on expectations of huge devaluations of their local currencies.

The resurgence of the shelters against the destruction of currencies by governments was not a novelty of 2016, but was accelerated with the generalization of financial-repression policies.

The search for ways to preserve wealth in a society which owns most of it in deposits makes citizens seek any way to avoid the assault on their savings from the massive printing of money through increase of money supply.

For this reason, the search for a currency whose control is not in the hands of States has been a constant in preserving capital for many years now.

Whenever government's imbalances soar, the "solution" almost inevitably comes from "dissolving" the wealth of citizens and appropriating it via inflation—the tax of the poor—and devaluation.

The difference between bitcoin and gold in recent years is basically that, while one has been rising fast as a possible currency and as a store of value, gold was seeing a more stable increase in value.

"Bitcoin is the beginning of something great: a currency without a government, something necessary and imperative." Nassim Taleb

Bitcoin is not yet a reality as a free currency for global use; its evolution depends on the ability to implement it globally and clarify doubts about its security against hackers and its value as a refuge.

Bitcoin is a currency start-up. A means of payment where States cannot interfere in the amount and cost of money available, where it is not possible to create fake money not backed by savings, and where one can "escape" and take refuge from the assault of central banks on the saver. Doubts come because the "shelter" is virtual and therefore always subject to computer attacks.

Bitcoin is proving to be a powerful exchange network and its revaluation shows that those who trust in that network maintain their positions in the medium term. As the increase in supply is limited, it is revalued in the face of increased demand.

A financial asset where its scarcity, future demand, and quality are valued against the possibility of exchanging it for other currencies, goods, or services in the future.

The fact that you can liquidate that asset and pay debts and taxes with the profits generated is positive. But it is not a currency until it can be used as a generally accepted means of payment for goods, services, taxes, and debts.

What bitcoin and the revaluation of the gold in 2016 showed us is that a growing part of the population continues to look for ways to shelter their savings against devaluations.

The Central Bank Trap and the Risk Hedge

At the end of this book, what I try to show is that even if the reader is a casual investor or a professional, we need to be used to the idea that:

- Believing that central banks will be there to shelter savers from risk does not work.
- Monetary policy may have succeeded in hiding the perception of risk, but accumulation is happening and volatility will rise.
- By definition, it does not make sense to find shelter from systemic risk by investing in the same assets that are accumulating such systemic risk.

Financial crises always happen due to the accumulation of exposure in assets that consensus and mainstream believe have little or no risk.

Economic cycles are not changed by macro policies, the effects of trying to cover imbalances with monetary laughing gas come back again with much more aggressiveness when credibility is lost.

Our Escape portfolio does not try to provide a one-stop solution for investors—that depends on their risk profile. There are no bad asset classes, just bad risk decisions when we deny cycles and decide to hold on for too long to winning bets.

That is one of the clearest mistakes that happen when we ignore that cycles are shorter, failing to take profits on good ideas.

Escape from the central bank trap can only be achieved by avoiding consensus bets and diversifying exposure so that our savings can be protected from the voracious appetite of inflationists.

A solid combination of sound fundamental bonds linked to inflation, rock-solid earnings and return-generating equities with maximum alignment of interests between shareholder and manager, and gold and alternative currencies, well diversified and managed actively, is, in my opinion, the best way to secure wealth and capital appreciation in this end of central-planned faith in alchemy.

Conclusion

The reader may have seen that this book is critical, but it is also hopeful and offers ideas based on pragmatism.

Central banks will continue to exist, and what I have tried to present here are ideas that some may share and others may not, but that can be implemented to cement credibility and avoid the enormous risk that is building up all over the world by denying the existence of bubbles and placing no interest in the rising tide of anger against mainstream monetary and economic policies.

The fact that there are risks should not preclude us from deciding to put our money to work, because if we do not, there is one certainty. Our savings will be worth less and less.

There is a tremendous opportunity for the world to show that financial operators, governments, and central banks can reorient their incentives to put their enormous power to reignite the growth of the middle class.

This growth of the middle class and improvement of the economy will come from a much more prudent approach to monetary policy: Make increasing disposable income the highest priority and let the private sector decide when and how investments should be made, allowing productive debt to overtake gratuitous deficit spending.

The central bank trap was not created in bad faith, and we must acknowledge that there have been some positives as we tried to note from the messages and policies of some of the governors. But the key message here is that we are dangerously close to crossing a line where uncertainty is taken over by panic and where citizens may simply lose any small element of trust in the system.

If panic was to arrive, it would catch central banks with no tools at all to mitigate the risk. Moving to negative rates after multiplying central bank balance sheets would not solve anything. Another QE after all that has been done would cause a total loss of faith in the system and blaming the wrong guys for the mistakes of policymakers.

It is time for supply-side policies and lower taxes and to allow companies to invest if they see opportunity, letting them seek those opportunities without constant bureaucracy burdens. Let families save, if they so desire, and consume the money they have earned working hard every day.

This will, in turn, lead to a more sustainable growth, where taxation is a means for improvement in public services, not a burden for growth and a perverse incentive to increase imbalances.

There are two sides to every story. The Keynesian reader may think that central banks have been the heroes of the crisis and that all the negatives happened due to reckless private companies. If that is the case, the Keynesian reader should also be alarmed at the insanely low bond yields and the amount of money created to generate such poor growth.

Whatever you want to believe, even if you still believe in "it would have been worse," "this time it's different," and "we have to repeat," there is one certainty.

The indiscriminate creation of money not supported by savings is always behind the greatest crises.

The escape from the Central Bank Trap is urgent.

It can be done in a way in which growth is stronger, citizens are better off, and perverse incentives are, at least, controlled.

Inflation is not an objective, it's an outcome.

Real productive investment is not decided by a committee that suffers no consequence if it fails.

Central Banks Don't Print Growth.

Let's rebuild the middle class.

London, January 2017

Endorsements

"Diocletian tried to combat inflation by fixing prices through laws. In reality, inflation was the product of the fiscal and monetary profligacy of the Roman emperors during the third century A. D. Dr. Daniel Lacalle's book exhibits how in the years after the global financial crisis, Governments and Central Banks have performed similar measures to those of the Roman emperors. This book shows the consequences of repeating past mistakes, and what can be done to limit such dire consequences."

—Ignacio de la Torre,
Professor and Academic Director at IE Business School.

"There is a Management model that I tried to explain to my students nationally and internationally. This model is based on the principles of subsidiarity, reciprocity and solidarity among people, business and policy makers. Lacalle's book *"Escape from the Central Bank"* explains in detail the consequences of massive intervention in the markets through monetary expansive measures, and why it is not the right way to proceed. This book is an absolutely must for those of us who believe in free markets and free society."

—Prof. Francisco J. Lara,
Busch School of Business, CUA Washington D.C.

"Researchers have written extensively on the topic of how money and monetary policy affect society and the international economy. Nevertheless, although the theory has been thoroughly examined, few best practices and recommendations have been put forward.

Each analyst has his or her individual point of view regarding the context that surrounds us. In his book Escape from the Central Bank Trap, the eminent economist and insightful thinker Dr. Daniel Lacalle reflects upon the most relevant internationally significant economic events of recent times. Lacalle conducts an original and visionary analysis that provides rich insights for evaluating future business decision made under high uncertainty. The value of this book is unquestionable; congratulations, Dr. Lacalle. Scholars, students, consultants, business managers, policy makers, and many others will find useful recommendations on the key issues dealt with in this book."

—Domingo Ribeiro-Soriano,
Professor of Business Administration, Universitat de València-Spain.

"In this book, Daniel Lacalle unveils, in a precise and clear way, proper uses (and misuses) of monetary policy and money creation, as perils associated to monetary gluts and what he coins as the "monetary laughing gas," when the healing power of monetary policies turns to be simply a placebo effect on the real economy. This challenging approach is particularly when potential imbalances fed by inconsistent policies hit a macroeconomic environment subject to hysteresis, reducing the room for maneuver in the future. In a transgressive way, he states that categories "conventional" or "unconventional" for monetary policy should be replaced by consistent (or not) policies, making monetary policy effectiveness depend mainly on its credibility and transparency."

—Juan Sapena,
Dean at Faculty of Economics, Catholic University of Valencia.

"To escape the trap of money printing, one has to understand why the trap didn't work to begin with. Lacalle is one of the leading next generation economists who can simplify the complex. He's neither a mainstream academic nor a flailing economic pundit. His teachings come from a market practitioner's perspective. This book is about the economic truth."

—Keith R. McCullough,
Chief Executive Officer, Hedgeye Risk Management.

"Escape from the Central Bank Trap provides a penetrating framework for understanding the co-dependencies among today's monetary policy, the economy and the financial markets. Lacalle's book draws out how these co-dependencies developed, the risks that have since evolved, and outlines the necessary tough medicine needed to return to a more sustainable condition. By distilling today's complex economic and monetary challenges succinctly, Lacalle provides us with a road map that an economist, market practitioner, or anyone who cares about long term economic health can grab hold of."

—Michael Purves,
Chief Global Strategist, WEEDEN & amp; CO.

"Professor Daniel Lacalle has done a wonderful job by providing a new interpretation of how central banks have contributed to worsening the financial crisis that we have all suffered during these recent years. Furthermore, the clarity of his explanations has provided a deeper understanding for practitioners and all those interested in monetary policy and its complex impact in the financial markets and the real economy. Ultimately, I do consider that this book will become essential reading material."

—Alvaro Martínez-Echevarría,
Dean and Director of the IEB Business School.

Bibliography

Apart from the scholar papers cited in the references.

Ahamed, Liaquat, Lords of Finance: 1929. *The Great Depression, and the Bankers Who Broke the World*. Penguin Press, 2009.

Bartholomew, James. *The Welfare of Nations*. Biteback Publishing, 2015.

Biggs, Barton. *Wealth, War and Wisdsom*. Wiley, 2009.

Bossidy, Larry, Charan Ram. Execution. *The Discipline of Getting Things Done*. Cron Business, 2006.

Butler, John. *The Golden Revolution*. Wiley, 2012.

Cooper, George. *The Origin of Financial Crises: Central Banks, Credit Bubbles and the Efficient Market Fallacy*. Harriman House, 2008.

Fabozzi, Frank J. *Bond Markets, Analysis and Strategies*. Pearson, 2006.

Hudson, Edward A. *Economic Growth: How It Works and How It Transformed the World*. Vernon, 2015.

Lewis, Michael, Boomerang. *Travels in the New Third World*. Norton.

Martin, Felix. *Money, the Unauthorized Biography*. Bodley.

Mauldin, John & Tepper, Jonathan. *Code Red*. Wiley, 2013.

Mills, Robin. *The Myth of the Oil Crisis*. Prager, 2013.

Ozihel, Harding. *Financial Repression*. Frac Press, 2012.

Pazos, Luis. *Desigualdad y distribución de la riqueza: Mitos y sofismas*. Diana México, 2016.

Reinhart, Carmen and Rogoff, Ken. *This Time Is Different: Eight Centuries of Financial Folly*. Princeton University Press, 2011.

Reinhart, Carmen and Rogoff, Ken. *A decade of debt*. Peterson Institute, 2011.

Schiff, Peter. *How an Economy Grows and Why It Crashes*. Wiley, 2010.

Sorkin, Andrew Ross. *Too Big to Fail: The Inside Story of How Wall Street and Washington Fought to Save the Financial System—and Themselves*. Penguin, 2011.

Straus, William, Howe, Neil. *The Fourth Turning*. Bantam Doubleday Dell, 1997.

Index

OTHER TITLES IN OUR FINANCE AND FINANCIAL MANAGEMENT COLLECTION

John A. Doukas, Old Dominion University, Editor

- *Money Laundering and Terrorist Financing Activities: A Primer on Avoidance Management for Money Managers* by Milan Frankl and Ayse Ebru Kurcer
- *Introduction to Foreign Exchange Rates, Second Edition* by Thomas J. O'Brien
- *Rays of Research on Real Estate Development* by Jaime Luque
- *Weathering the Storm: The Financial Crisis and the EU Response, Volume I: Background and Origins of the Crisis* by Javier Villar Burke
- *Weathering the Storm: The Financial Crisis and the EU Response, Volume II: The Response to the Crisis* by Javier Villar Burke
- *Rethinking Risk Management: Critically Examining Old Ideas and New Concepts* by Rick Nason
- *Towards a Safer World of Banking: Bank Regulation After the Subprime Crisis* by T.T. Ram Mohan
- *The Penny Share Millionaire: The Ultimate Guide to Trading* by Jacques Magliolo

Announcing the Business Expert Press Digital Library

Concise e-books business students need for classroom and research

This book can also be purchased in an e-book collection by your library as

- a one-time purchase,
- that is owned forever,
- allows for simultaneous readers,
- has no restrictions on printing, and
- can be downloaded as PDFs from within the library community.

Our digital library collections are a great solution to beat the rising cost of textbooks. E-books can be loaded into their course management systems or onto students' e-book readers.
The **Business Expert Press** digital libraries are very affordable, with no obligation to buy in future years. For more information, please visit **www.businessexpertpress.com/librarians**. To set up a trial in the United States, please email **sales@businessexpertpress.com**.

CPSIA information can be obtained
at www.ICGtesting.com
Printed in the USA
BVHW041349260620
582324BV00006B/440

9 781631 577833